TWAYNE'S WORLD AUTHORS SERIES

A Survey of the World's Literature

Sylvia E. Bowman, Indiana University

GENERAL EDITOR

GREECE

Mary Gianos, Detroit Institute of Technology

EDITOR

Plutarch

(*TWAS 111*)

TWAYNE'S WORLD AUTHORS SERIES (TWAS)

The purpose of TWAS is to survey the major writers —novelists, dramatists, historians, poets, philosophers, and critics—of the nations of the world. Among the national literatures covered are those of Australia, Canada, China, Eastern Europe, France, Germany, Greece, India, Italy, Japan, Latin America, New Zealand, Poland, Russia, Scandinavia, Spain, and the African nations, as well as Hebrew, Yiddish, and Latin Classical literatures. This survey is complemented by Twayne's United States Authors Series and English Authors Series.

The intent of each volume in these series is to present a critical analytical study of the works of the writer; to include biographical and historical material that may be necessary for understanding, appreciation, and critical appraisal of the writer; and to present all material in clear, concise English—but not to vitiate the scholarly content of the work by doing so.

Plutarch

By C. J. GIANAKARIS

Western Michigan University

Twayne Publishers Inc. :: New York

Library of Congress Catalog Number: 78–120499

ABOUT THE AUTHOR

C. J. Gianakaris, one of the founding editors of the international quarterly *Comparative Drama,* is the editor of *Antony and Cleopatra* in the Blackfriars Shakespeare series. He has published in many journals, including *College English, JEGP, The Huntington Library Quarterly, Drama Survey,* and *The Western Humanities Review.* His A.B. and M.A. degrees were earned at the University of Michigan. He received the Ph.D. in English in 1961 from the University of Wisconsin, where he wrote a disertation on the humanism of Ben Jonson. Currently associate professor of English at Western Michigan University, Dr. Gianakaris also has taught at Illinois State University.

For
my three Anns

PLUTARCH

by

C. J. GIANAKARIS

To many readers today Plutarch is recognized as a source for Shakespeare's Roman tragedies or as the biographer of certain Greek and Roman heroes from antiquity. But beyond this popular reputation stands his larger significance as the foremost spokesman of Western man's classical heritage. Born in the first century after Christ, Plutarch represents an intellectual paradox. Though he created no innovative philosophy of his own, in his commentaries he passed along the essence of many profound philosophies. Though he did not write fictional works, he retold countless tales of intrigue in his narratives, thereby preserving the stories of others for future generations. And though he denied himself the title of historian, his accounts of persons and events constitute one of our richest, most valuable portrayals of life in ancient times. This book is intended to examine Plutarch's humanistic nature and the impact his works have had on the most noteworthy writers since his death. When his achievement is viewed as a whole, it becomes obvious that Plutarch has successfully bridged two thousand years to live among us today, the thoughtful scholar whose respect for man's capabilities mirrors that of humanists of all eras.

Acknowledgments

My thanks go to Harvard University Press for permission to quote liberally from the Loeb Classical Library editions of Plutarch's *Parallel Lives* and the *Moralia;* also for *Emerson's Plutarch,* by Edmund G. Berry.

To Random House, Inc., for the Modern Library Giant *Plutarch's Lives.*

To Chatto and Windus (in London) and Indiana Univesrsity Press for *Plutarch and His Times,* by R. H. Barrow.

To Barnes & Noble, Inc., for *The Classical Background of English Literature,* by J. A. K. Thomson.

I wish to offer my gratitude to the Classics Library at the University of Illinois, to Milner Library at Illinois State University, to Waldo Library at Western Michigan University, and to Kelsey Museum at the University of Michigan.

Also, my thanks to Illinois State University for three faculty research grants and to Western Michigan University for one research grant, all of which assisted me in this undertaking.

Finally, my special appreciation to Professor Mary P. Gianos for her helpful editorial work with this manuscript.

Preface

Once to be introduced to Plutarch is to love him always. This book proposes to offer a balanced introduction for such love and appreciation to flourish.

Only a hundred years ago, when the classics were central in an educated person's training, many of the details brought out here would have been common knowledge. Regarding Plutarch and his immense influence on subsequent eras, the classicist J. A. K. Thomson believes that "It is hardly an exaggeration to say that at least up to the nineteenth century the picture of ancient Greece and Rome in the modern mind was the picture painted by him." Today, a reader must make a more conscious effort to inform himself of the full dimensions of Plutarch as an intellectual figure and of his impact on the civilized world. That effort is well worth the trouble, as this book sets out to prove.

Early in our study, the matter of Plutarch's categorization as an author is examined. The issue arises in the first place because he accomplished so much of a varied nature during his lifetime. He is recognized by many readers as the foremost biographer from antiquity. There seems little doubt that it is through the *Parallel Lives* that he is best known to present generations. Yet, notwithstanding occasional outcries from a few purists, Plutarch also is seen to be a successful historian because he so effectively revives the ethos of ancient times. Another facet of this Greek writer has impressed readers of every epoch, the commonsense morality which pervades all that he wrote. In this connection, one discovers in his works the outlines of several key schools of philosophy from antiquity, such as Platonism, neo-Platonism, Aristotelianism, and Stoicism, among them. Although he does not formulate a unique philosophy for himself, Plutarch alludes openly and often to the best known systems of others, a point remarked upon in Chapter 5 of this book. Nor do Plutarch's talents cease at this point.

Throughout his *Moralia* and the *Lives*, the sole bodies of his writings left to us, one encounters an incredible assortment of tales concerning renowned personages and important events in history already ancient in his own day. From this perspective, Plutarch appears an observer and chronicler, much like a columnist in our modern monthly journals.

Thorough readers of Plutarch therefore discover that he filled a variety of roles as biographer, historian, moralist, philosopher, and general observer of men's manners. Common to each of his occupations (or preoccupations) was his remarkable sensitivity to characters and happenings. All his life he was exceptionally alert to people and what they did, whether of his own lifetime or recorded in the past. What he observed or read he either burned into his memory or else jotted down as notes in the notebooks which always accompanied him. His fortuitous visits in Rome as guest lecturer provided him with the occasions to codify his random observations, readings, and philosophical meditations, products derived from his humanistic upbringing. The sum total of his writings has come to be of enormous significance to subsequent generations, chiefly because his commentaries of famed persons and events represent a rich compendium of stories and details from the past. In the final analysis, as this study will indicate, Plutarch's finest achievement has been to serve as an essential intellectual and literary transmission channel from antiquity. The final two chapters of this book are designed to reveal our immeasurable debt to Plutarch at large.

By far the most useful clue to Plutarch as man and as thinker is his humanism. Nothing that he wrote fell outside the pale of humanistic doctrine. Our opening chapter tells of his background and how his family and education encouraged his innate respect for the capacities of mankind. The fourth and fifth chapters reveal the results of that indoctrination, by our quoting freely from his own writings on many subjects. Although his announced intention to trace men's lives in combined historical-biographical fashion remains the central design for the *Parallel Lives*, Plutarch never evades an ethical, humanistic orientation in his essays. He describes the personal benefits he derived from setting down the *Lives* in this passage:

For the result is like nothing else than daily living and associating together, when I receive and welcome each subject of my history in turn as my guest, so to speak, and observe carefully "how large he was and of what mien," and select from his career what is most important and most beautiful to know. (*Life of Timoleon,* LCL Vol. VI, Chapter I, 261)

Chapter 2 of this book establishes the humanistic core underlying his appraisals of the lives led by his subjects. More precisely, that core is comprised of a firm bond coupling self-discipline and human reason. Together they can lead to what the ancient Greeks called the good life, if the ultimate universal forces permit. For maximum success in leading life properly, Plutarch insisted, both parties, human and supernatural, must cooperate in the venture.

One further consideration needs to be brought into focus: the singular good fortune that attended Plutarch's career. At first glance, it would seem unlucky to have been born a Greek when he was, at a time when Greece's finest days were over and she stood simply as a minor province in the Roman sphere of influence. The surface chronology is misleading, however, as the first chapter here attempts to make clear. In truth, Plutarch was fortunate both in his family and in his moment in history. Because his family enjoyed relative wealth, a long-standing heritage, and community respect, Plutarch was enabled to receive a superior education, along with many opportunities to participate in civic administration at Chaeronea. Because shrunken Greece no longer represented a military threat by then, Rome could afford to display a liberal attitude toward Greece's last remaining commodity of true value, her intellectual spokesmen. Moreover, the Romans still were reaping the relatively pacific rewards of the *Pax Romanox,* on the eve of her own gradual decline from world rule. For these and other reasons, five of Rome's leaders during the decades of Plutarch's lifetime could sympathize with (and covet) Greek thought and culture. As a consequence, Plutarch eventually was sponsored by Rome to lecture and write, not by Greece. All these bits of luck converged in Plutarch, we shall see.

As it turned out, Plutarch's good fortune continued on after his death. In light of the majority of other authors from antiquity whose efforts were lost entirely during the dark ages, he must be considered singularly blessed. Nearly half his work was preserved, we now estimate. Among the earliest sources, for instance, we still have the Greek Anthology, which includes some of his brief statements. At the same time, various Church fathers also helped to perpetuate many of his ethical discourses. Of far greater importance to modern times was Jacques Amyot's splendid French translation of Plutarch's works, first of the *Lives* in the mid-1500s, and later that century of the *Moralia.* So complete was Amyot's success in delivering these writings into Renaissance Europe that his translations have become paradigms for all later translators. With Amyot's version available on the Continent, Plutarch gained new impetus among readers who were not comfortable in the classical languages. Relatively uneducated commoners became intrigued by his colorful tales of past heroes. Meanwhile, Renaissance religious leaders, like their predecessors, found much appropriate material for their sermons in the didactic portions of the *Moralia.* Furthermore, Amyot's translation of the *Parallel Lives* led directly to a second windfall for Plutarch, when Thomas North translated Amyot's French version into English during the 1570s. Since they existed in the vernacular for Europeans at the crest of the Renaissance, Plutarch's works gained the extra advantage of the special concern in antiquity which thrived at that moment. Shakespeare became one of a score of exceedingly influential authors coming under Plutarch's spell as a result of the ready accessibility of his writings. Chapter 6 makes an effort to set these details in proper perspective and to convey the fortuitous circumstances which helped to assist Plutarch's work through the centuries following his death.

The present study, to emphasize, holds as its primary objective the introduction of Plutarch to as many readers as possible in the modern era. Emerging from this book are defining attributes, such as his congeniality, his learnedness, and his didactic humanism, which constitute his principal hallmarks. The fact that his temperament and attitudes are not alien to many humanists alive now will also emerge on its own. Last, in keeping with the intentions of this book, it should be noted that the author has employed a simplified system for citing excerpts from the *Parallel Lives* and the *Moralia.* As indicated in Chapter 2, almost all quotations from Plutarch are taken from the Loeb Classical Library editions (abbreviated as LCL). The particular *Life* or essay under discussion is cited first by title, followed by section or chapter number in the particular LCL volume, and completed by the page reference. In a related decision, the bibliography offered at the conclusion of the book is limited to works in English, with only a very few exceptions; for this reason, most books listed therein should be available to readers in many libraries. These are arbitrary stylistic decisions, no doubt. But the author firmly believes that the words of Plutarch must be brought to contemporary readers in as unencumbered fashion as possible. To live on, the Sage of Chaeronea must be read; and to be read, Plutarch's writings must be available in a convenient format.

C. J. GIANAKARIS

Kalamazoo, Michigan

Contents

Chronology

A.D.

c. 46 Plutarch was born into an old family of wealth in Chaeronea, a small town halfway between Athens and Delphi in the province of Boeotia (also the natal home of Pindar). Plutarch's immediate family included his brothers Timon and Lamprias, his father (believed to be named Autobulus), his mother (whose name is not known), and a grandfather called Lamprias whom Plutarch mentions several times in his writings.

c. 66 As a youth Plutarch went to Athens to secure a humanistic education built around studies in rhetoric, physics, mathematics, medicine, the natural sciences, philosophy, and Greek and Latin literatures. Ammonius of Lamptrae, it is thought, was Plutarch's tutor, accounting for Plutarch's strong neo-Platonic bias and wide religious knowledge. To cap his education, the young Plutarch broadened himself by traveling widely in Greece, Asia Minor, and Alexandria in Egypt.

c. 68 While yet a young man, Plutarch married Timoxena who was to bear him four sons—Soclarus, Chairon, Autobulus, and Plutarchus—and one daughter called Timoxena. Only two of their children, Autobulus and Plutarchus, were still living at the time of Plutarch's death. After obtaining his education, Plutarch returned to Chaeronea to become a public servant. He served there as a teacher and also as the town's official representative to the Roman governor.

70s Plutarch's elevation in rank while serving his community led to occasional diplomatic missions in Rome. While an emissary to Rome, he made contacts and close friends among important dignitaries, resulting in his being invited to lecture all around Italy (in Greek, the learned man's language in Rome) on philosophy and moral matters.

80s Upon returning to his homeland from his lectures in Rome, Plutarch apparently began shaping his extensive notebooks and his observations into essays—probably the beginning pieces in what became his *Moralia*.

90s Plutarch's second sojourn in Rome and elsewhere in Italy took place during these years. This time, his lecture tours, which lasted a few years, proved to be even greater successes than before, because by now he was a celebrated man of philosophy and letters. His audiences were large and friendly. During these years, even though he was a member of a subjugated people within a Roman dynasty, Plutarch enjoyed the encouragement of Rome. Five emperors during Plutarch's lifetime were known for their pro-Hellenic attitudes—Nero, Vespasian, Domitian, Trajan, and Hadrian. The warmth with which Plutarch was received in Rome and the popularity of his writings must be attributed to the favorable intellectual climate then prevailing for learned Greeks within the Empire.

c. 99–120 Plutarch concluded his second lecture tour in Rome somewhat suddenly (*c.* 99) and returned to his native Chaeronea. There, he assumed a variety of civic positions, both of high and low level: he served as archon in Chaeronea, as director of the games during special festivals, and as chairman (*proedros*) of the Amphictyonic Council which traditionally met at Delphi. Of greater significance was Plutarch's becoming head priest at Delphi, a post he held for the last twenty years of his life. His administration at Delphi proved so successful that the near moribund condition of the Temple was reversed to keep the oracle a viable influence for a few additional years. Most scholars believe that Plutarch wrote most of the *Lives* and some sections of the *Moralia* during these latter busy years of his life.

c. 120 Plutarch died a peaceful death, an old man fully occupied with assisting Greece and his fellow man in accordance with his strongly held humanistic tenets. The Boeotians so appreciated Plutarch's efforts on their behalf that they dedicated an inscription to him at Delphi—one which remains and can be seen yet today.

CHAPTER 1

The Life and Age of Plutarch

If thou art minded any pagan soul
From threatened doom to save, O Christ of mine,
Plato and Plutarch save, and please me well.[1]

SUCH words of reverence for the pagans Plutarch and Plato, written during the eleventh century by the church dignitary John Metropolitan of Euchaita, can only suggest the continued respect and affection which the civilized world has maintained for Plutarch. The eminent classical scholar J. A. K. Thomson today unhesitatingly claims Plutarch to be "one of the most influential writers who ever lived,"[2] a viewpoint readily supported by an awesome listing of the renowned in history who are directly indebted to Plutarch—among others, Montaigne, Shakespeare, Corneille, Racine, Jonson, Napoleon, Heine, Rousseau, Shelley, Melville, and Emerson.

Precisely what makes Plutarch appealing for the multitudes attracted to him down the centuries is partly clear and partly puzzling. That a dramatist like Shakespeare should lift, virtually unaltered, several of his Roman heroes from Plutarch's accounts reflects the biographer's usefulness to a writing craftsman seeking to mirror absorbing yet human figures, a fact we shall explore in detail later. At the same time, generally speaking, historians hold cavalier attitudes toward Plutarch, insisting that as a promulgator of historical data he fails rather badly. His facts often are claimed to be inaccurate, especially those concerning historical events, which they deem to be colored by personal bias. None refutes the notion, however, that Plutarch's personality shows through in his writings, thereby instilling a unique quality of human-ness rarely found in authors of any era. This ability to view all events in the world in terms of human qualities (motivation and character, for instance) is Plutarch's special hallmark, pleasing most general readers while frustrating historians.

I *Establishing a Perspective for Plutarch and His Era*

In any consideration of Plutarch it is essential to state early that complete certainty regarding facts of his life and deeds is not ours to enjoy. One of the most verbose biographers of the ancient world, who expended an infinite number of words on others, never decided to record his own life in a formal autobiography. Furthermore, Plutarch's contemporaries remained reticent about him. What we now know concerning Plutarch's life has been pieced together from allusions to himself and his family which do appear in his works. Additionally, to our good fortune, recently discovered epigraphs speak explicitly of honors accorded Plutarch, such as honorary consular rank in Rome. These testify to his actions and to the admiration people held for him. Ultimately, too, we have the most crucial substance of all, his voluminous writings themselves in which his personal ethical criteria are displayed continuously. Using these materials as our base we are enabled to reconstruct a reasonably accurate and sensitive profile of Plutarch.

Equally imperative in comprehending Plutarch, the man and writer, is taking into account the fact of his historical and geographical milieu. Ironically, this author who has left us vital portraits of grand deeds and protagonists of antiquity himself was the product of a stifled, conquered land, no longer enjoying any influence over its own destiny. When he was born about A.D. 46 in the Greek state of Boeotia, Plutarch entered a world whose civilized portions were predominantly Roman. The extraordinary Golden Age of Greece of the fourth and fifth centuries B.C. had gradually dissipated until by Plutarch's era the country suffered from uniform poverty and collapse of autonomy. A look backward in time to about the second and third centuries B.C. is sufficient to suggest the many causes involved in the eventual decline of Hellas. Scholars of today, such as M. Rostovtzeff (*The Social & Economic History of the Hellenistic World*, 3 vols., Oxford, 1941), have documented the unsettling factors which had always plagued Greeks and which had prohibited any ultimate accommodation among the individual city-states. Whether one places primary guilt on the cynical coalition of the kings and the leaders of the cities or on the opportunistic strategies of the Romans who were gradually encroaching on Greece, the fact remains that the various city-states were materially and morally drained by constant turmoil, internal and external. Two hundred years before Plutarch's birth, the disintegration of the once grand and proud land of the Greeks began in earnest. As Rostovtzeff describes the situation, "In the atmosphere of war, of organized brigandage and common rapine, of confiscations and requisitions, life in Greece was utterly disorganized. Demoralization seized upon both the upper and the lower classes, and social unrest, disturbances, and revolutions were of ordinary occurrence." Interestingly enough, Rostovtzeff adds that, in Plutarch's native province during the second century B.C., "class antagonism reached its highest pitch in Boeotia."

Polybius, the second century B.C. Greek historian, commented fully on one result of Greece's long-standing upheaval, her depopulation. Although no concrete figures have been left to the modern world concerning the exact numbers of people living in a single city-state of Hellas, enough observers at the time recorded that as Greece's power waned, its hold on population similarly diminished. Steadily down to and through the era of Plutarch, Hellas suffered from a worsening case of manpower malnutrition. When, therefore, Plutarch made his often-quoted statement about leaving Rome to remain in his impoverished native town "so that it should not become even less," he was not speaking strictly in jest.

Related to the matter of shifting population centers is that of economics. Whereas at its summit the Hellenic states could boast handsome temples, theaters, halls, and palaces adorned with superlative Greek statuary and frescoes, they found their monies being spent in maintaining wars and in offsetting a growing unfavorable balance of trade.[3] And of course once they eventually committed themselves to joining with Mithridates against the Romans following their earlier debilitating insurrections of the first century B.C., the Hellenes assured themselves crushing retaliation with the incumbent plundering, pillage, and devastation.[4]

By the time of Plutarch's birth, Pericles and the mighty attainments of a flourishing Hellenic peoples had largely receded into blurring memories. Greece had experienced nearly 250 years of Roman rule by then, hardening her for the almost two thousand years of subjugation to follow until an eventual release from the Turks in the nineteenth century. Though we cannot document with any finiteness the reasons that caused Greece to continue two thousand years in a mesmerized state, one fascinating theory, Greece's brain drain, would seem to account for the phenomenon. According to that view, when the Hellenic states were paramount —say under Alexander—they were skimming off the intellectual cream from the homeland, sending them to newly conquered lands to proselytize and instruct. Unwittingly, they consequently deprived Greece of the very same intelligent and virile youth necessary to sustain any viable national structure. The Greek didactic impulse in this instance may have resulted in the Hellenes spreading themselves too thin. But such conjecture remains a topic for another time.

II *Plutarch's Family Heritage and His Youth*

Plutarch's birthplace of Chaeronea, at any event, if not at the hub of Greek activity during the earlier Hellenistic period nonetheless had notable history associated with its name. Situated in the province of Boeotia halfway between Athens and the long-renowned town of Delphi, Plutarch's village also had served as the natal home for Pindar and Epaminondas in earlier days. Less happily recalled, too, Chaeronea was the site of Mithridates' final defeat. Considering the general state of Hellas at the time, however, Plutarch was particularly fortunate in his birth. Although we cannot be certain as to the original sources for the wealth, it is beyond dispute that Plutarch's family was an old one, having a tradition of at least moderate affluence behind it.[5] Inscriptions suggest, to illustrate, that his family members for generations had held civic positions of authority in the region of Chaeronea. Plutarch along with his parents and his brothers Lamprias and Timon lived on a family estate where income from the land and its goods provided them with a not uncomfortable existence. Lending support to their well-to-do status are apocryphal stories which turn up, alluding to Plutarch's keeping of slaves and to his aristocratic attitudes toward them.

Possessed of sufficient funds, Plutarch was able to enjoy the best kind of education available to a Greek youth in those hard-pressed days. Athens remained even in Plutarch's age the most attractive university town for both Greeks and Romans,[6] and it was there that he went to pursue the standard humanistic curriculum: rhetoric, physics, mathematics, natural sciences, medicine, and what can best be called by the general term philosophy. By his own admission, it was the last discipline which held the greatest attraction for Plutarch, and it was his tutor, Ammonius of Lamptrae, who steeped the young man in neo-Platonism. In addition, Ammonius was considered a very learned man in the realm of religious knowledge. It is not surprising therefore that traces of his mentor's religio-moralistic approach to philosophy and life were to be apparent in all Plutarch later was to write. Apparent also in Plutarch's essays was his remarkable knowledge of Greek literature and earlier Latin books. The abundance of quotations and paraphrased statements in his writings reflects both an awesome memory and a well-crammed notebook. In his *Parallel Lives* alone he quotes from more than two hundred writers,[7] an even more incredible feat when one considers that printed texts were not available and that purchasing manuscripts was difficult and costly.[8]

Nor was his knowledge restricted to book learning. In keeping with the conventional genteel education throughout recorded history, Plutarch traveled extensively, both in and out of Greece proper. Aside from longer sojourns in Rome and elsewhere on the Italian peninsula, Plutarch made trips to Asia Minor, Alexandria in Egypt, and an assortment of widely separated Greek towns, such as Sparta, Tanagra, Plataea, Patrae, Aedepsus, Thermopylae, Thespiae, Elis, and Helicon, to name only a few.[9]

At some time during his younger years Plutarch met and married a woman named Timoxena, who by all accounts displayed great common sense as well as devotion to her husband. When their sole daughter, also called Timoxena, died at four years of age, Plutarch was prompted to write his well-known letter of condolence to his wife; at the time he was away from home on a mission. In our later consideration of that letter, we shall see traces of Stoicism in both Plutarch's thought and his wife's courage in the face of a painful loss. From time to time in his writings Plutarch also mentions his other children, four boys named Soclarus, Chairon, Autobulus, and Plutarchus. Only the last two were to survive their parents. Other family members also appear by name in Plutarch's essays. Recurrent are names like Nicarchus, a great-grandfather, Lamprias, Plutarch's grandfather, and Autobulus, generally conceded to be the name of his father. Most assuredly, therefore, Plutarch was heir to a fine family tradition (which he was to pass on unblemished), a strong academic training, and a gentleman's firsthand knowledge of the world and its peoples, thanks to extensive travel.

III *A Greek in a Roman World*

Only Plutarch's status as a citizen of an occupied realm would hinder his personal career or that of an equally qualified countryman. With Greece enjoying no political or economic leverage under the *Pax Romana,* severe limitations understandably were placed on any young ambitious Greek. In addition to the huge costs of the ceaseless warring, the Greeks had prohibitive tributes to pay their Roman victors, a bleeding process which necessarily decimated the treasuries of the states and temples. Without her former wealth and abundant credit, the Hellenic business enterprises in turn disappeared, dissolving with them opportunities for advancement in the world of commerce. The remnants of Greece's earlier manufacturing and merchandising constituted but a smaller part of the Roman economic complex. Conducting any significant business ventures independent of Rome consequently was out of the question. The legendary merchant marine fleets of the Greeks no longer probed the ports of the world on behalf of Grecian states but rather shuttled Roman goods back and forth across the broad Roman domain for Roman entrepreneurs.

Hopes for a sparkling life in the business realm were thus out of the question in his day for even a well-bred, well-educated Greek like Plutarch. Numbed, humiliated, and made benign by poverty, shrunken Hellas served no vital role in the grand Roman blueprint being unrolled. Roads, villages, and populations withered; herding sheep became—and remained for centuries—the major vocation accessible to a Greek. Though they never were to relinquish entirely their so-called Greek character, the Hellenes within the context of a world Roman on all sides gradually came to assimilate the customs of their conquerors. By the time of Constantine the Great, the Greeks were even to call themselves *Romaioi,* or citizens of the new Rome, suggesting that Greece's historical identity was being absorbed into the more viable existence of Rome, if not eradicated by that power.[10]

When Plutarch had completed the formal part of his education, consequently, he looked out at a Roman cosmos. Whereas the bickering Greek peoples could only rarely concur long enough to consolidate into any kind of unified political entity, the Romans in seizing the land enforced a peace. Thus, though finally at peace and in one sense united, the Hellenes found themselves powerless and out of the world's limelight. Chaeronea, Plutarch's native town, stood as an insignificant speck within the wide-reaching boundaries of the Empire. Rome at that moment was enjoying its uppermost plateau of prominence, Hadrian's realm exceeding in breadth the whole of continental United States today. Its borders encompassed Spain in the west and all the land east to Parthia, and in the north the land comprising the British Isles of today south through the upper tier of countries along the Mediterranean coastline of Africa.

Were he empowered to look beyond his own immediate age, Plutarch ultimately could have witnessed the fragmentation of the phenomenal power and resources which had constituted the Roman universe. Just as Greece could not sustain its position, Rome followed a downhill path but then in accordance with an entirely different set of circumstances. As historians never tire of informing us, the Empire carried within it the seeds of its own doom. Economic historians today, to illustrate, suggest that Rome eventually fell to the Barbarians about the fourth century A.D. because it failed to develop "systematically its own economic resources." [11] A longer-standing tradition, on the other hand, has it that moral decay from within made the Roman achievement susceptible to conquest from without. The Empire could not camouflage its own infections, vicious in-fighting, and increasing degradation of spirit and moral integrity, as Gibbon and others testify. As a result, it now has become a commonplace to hear about "the wholesale wallowing in sex and food and drink at Rome." [12]

Nor were Rome's inhabitants at the time oblivious to the state of affairs. Latin satirists joined philosophers in Plutarch's era to condemn the rank crimes and cruelties. "A black and shameful age" is Tacitus' verdict,[13] while Juvenal decries the "cruelty shown to slaves, the unbridled sexuality of the new women," which to him proved Rome encouraged violence as a way of life.[14] Though the putting down of the last Greek uprising in 31 B.C. at Actium was to usher in the celebrated Roman Peace, it simultaneously was to mark the commencement of Rome's eventual deterioration. As early as Augustus' tenure as *princeps* around 23 B.C., the issue of flagging morality was perceptible. Augustus, to illustrate, went so far as to seek to upgrade Roman ethical behavior by reinstituting a state religion.[15]

Epitomizing the more prevailing attitude of Imperial Rome, however, was the bizarre Nero who, though responsible for a few laudable deeds during his lifetime, yet aided substantially in promulgating the indecencies of the times. Nero's one-time personal minion Petronius, in a single work like *The Satyricon*, draws an unforgettably lucid, even if obscene, portrait of the shocking epoch. Fratricide, internecine murders, savagery in the arena, licentiousness beyond sadistic perversion—such growing characteristics of Roman society were flailed repeatedly by scornful commentators of the time. Another rather different kind of associate of Nero, Seneca, who also was contemporary with Plutarch, in his *Moral Essays* sums up the feelings of sensitive intellectuals in confessing that "one is sometimes seized by hatred of the whole human race." [16]

It was not Plutarch's lot to witness the eventual disintegration and collapse of Rome, a process extending by stages over several centuries. Since he died about A.D. 120, he saw none of the final agonies of Rome leading to the ultimate crisis late in the fifth century. In fact, as we shall be observing, Plutarch saw little at all in Rome to elicit anything but praise for the state.

Despite the multitude of culpable deeds committed by the Romans in Plutarch's day, they should be credited with at least one redeeming quality, a pro-Hellenic attitude concerning Greece's intellectual and artistic culture. Without attempting to exonerate gross acts by the Imperial heads, we need to recognize that the general phil-Hellenic position held by most of them permitted many Greek intellectuals to live peaceful, even successful, lives. It is true that the Romans had no patience for Greece's political institutions and theories. Why should they, in view of the inept political debacles perpetuated by various Hellenic city-states? But the cultural heritage of that same Greek civilization was another matter. Though the form of Roman esteem for Greek art might take a destructive turn—as when, for example, emperors had Greek temples ransacked to obtain statuary for adorning edifices in Rome—it was commonplace for the Romans to import large numbers of Greek artisans, writers, and philosophers to enhance and glorify the new hub of the civilized world. The classicist Gilbert Murray offers an acute assessment when claiming that

"Greece became essentially the paid teacher of the Roman world." [17]

Far from holding the captive Greek nations in ignominious bondage, once it was clear that the Hellenes no longer posed any military threat, the Roman leaders swung over in quite the opposite direction, displaying overt bias toward everything Hellenic. As a result Plutarch was enabled to lead the fruitful life he did and the satellite province of Greece could continue offering the cultured world something productive, at least for a while longer.

To underscore these facts, one may observe that of the nine emperors holding power during Plutarch's life span, five were actively pro-Hellenic, specifically Nero (54-68), Vespasian (69-79), Domitian (81-96), Trajan (98-117), and particularly Hadrian (117-38).[18] Although in those times an educated Greek could not aspire to positions of supreme authority within the Roman world, Plutarch was not so badly treated. The Hellenic intellectuals were welcomed warmly by the culture-seeking patrons of Rome. A thoughtful observer of the era has commented that "Greeks came to have the same standing as Latin-speaking provincials in the eyes of the imperial government. In Rome a Greek author received the same recognition as his Roman confrere. Greek historians, geographers, scientists, rhetoricians, and philosophers wrote not only for Greeks but for the educated circles of the whole Empire." [19]

IV *Forging a Career as Diplomat and Scholar*

Although it was not to be long before Plutarch's talents would become enmeshed with Roman affairs, he commenced his illustrious productive years in his homeland. Upon completing his formal education while yet a young man, Plutarch returned to Chaeronea to pursue the multifaceted career best suited to a humanist of the age. At home he became a public servant, a teacher, and simply a civic dignitary in general. For a time he served in a minor capacity as Chaeronea's representative to the Roman governor whose province included that section of Greece. Years later, Plutarch was to comment on those early years as an emissary sometimes sent to Rome on minor assignments. Psychologically, one could easily trace Plutarch's humility in later life to such training during his formative years. In one recollection of those days, he mentions that he had to bear the principal burden in some diplomatic negotiations when his superior faltered. Yet, when the young Plutarch returned to Greece and began relating the episode before others as his own successful venture, his father interrupted to insist that he use "we" in his account and thus share the credit with his inept cohort.

As elsewhere in his career, no complete picture can be assembled. The explicit details we have at this point are often contradictory and unreliable. We may assume with some safety, though, that Plutarch's tenure as occasional envoy to Rome on behalf of his home district led to his making important contacts in the heart of the Empire. Two rather prolonged sojourns in Rome are not in dispute, the first during the seventies and the second during the nineties. Nor can we rule out still other visits there. The exact nature of his business while in Rome cannot be ascertained on the basis of concrete evidence, unfortunately. Still it is very likely that any diplomatic missions involved were subordinated to Plutarch's lectures before growing gatherings of Romans. If Plutarch were but a young man with no impressive reputation during his earlier extended visit in the seventies, the same cannot be said for the second trip when his renown was assured; by then his learned writings had been completed.[20]

The fact that Plutarch was spoken of as a philosopher while touring Rome and what we now call Italy does not necessarily mean he propounded formal philosophical systems in his lectures. As we noticed before, the term "philosophy" was employed in a rather loose sense at the time. Probably his discussions can best be likened to quasihistorical and personal narrative built on a firm moralistic base. The lectures he delivered while in Rome later were to comprise a large portion of his *Moralia,* since he continued to collect his views all his lifetime. Our exploration of the *Moralia* later will offer ample testament to the casual and long-term nature of those pieces. Plutarch drew large gatherings to his speeches and forums, a fact which he mentions on more than one occasion in his essays. Much like the visiting scholar on a campus today, he was received with respect by his listeners. He was invited into the homes of dignitaries wherever he stopped, in some cases establishing firm friendships with his Roman hosts, as many of his dedications to them indicate. To sum up, Plutarch made his mark with his lectures and should be seen as a celebrity in certain intellectual circles.[21]

For Plutarch, his sojourns in the geographic center of the gigantic Roman domain proved gratifying; large attendances appeared at his talks in which he explicated individual and public morality. It must be assumed as a consequence that his auditors were interested in the issues raised by his topics. Strangely shadowing his obvious pleasant view of Roman life and providing a contrast is the cynical picture of Rome depicted by the satirists of that age, as we observed earlier. The scenes of everyday life found in the writings of a Juvenal or the debauched Petronius overflow with ugliness and degeneracy. Any page selected at random from Petronius' *The Satyricon* will serve to illustrate.

That Plutarch's pronouncements of the same Rome of the same era should prove as sanguine as Petronius' are disillusioned and jaded may be paradoxical but understandable. Plutarch, after all, was being guided around Rome as a visiting lecturer from abroad, staying at the homes of Roman elite who had befriended him. They surely would have no cause to point out the seamy side of their city or the flaws of their society to an intellectual of a conquered people. Add to this the fact that Plutarch was not exposed to everyday conversations of average Roman citizens. He both wrote and spoke in Greek while in Rome, because at the time he had not yet studied Latin sufficiently to converse in it with any facility.[22] The Greek language, we need to remind ourselves, remained the official vehicle for the written and spoken expression of Roman intellectuals, even though it was Greece that had been conquered by Rome. In this circumstance, therefore, he would be impressed by the deference shown him by his hosts while also being oblivious to the commonplace crudities in the life of Rome beneath its surface; the latter remains a truism valid today for any tourist to a strange land.

For Plutarch, Rome shone at best advantage. He was a celebrated thinker come to share his knowledge while being attended by the congenial aristocracy of the hub of the Empire. One can accuse him neither of blindness to social ills nor of nefarious motives in his calling Rome "fairest of all the works in mankind," even though his judgment stands in sharp contrast to the shocking descriptions by the satirical epigrammatists actually leading their lives there.

Similarly, one can logically account for what appears to be a gross incongruity of facts regarding his renown in Rome, if all the factors are considered. An occasional scholar of Plutarch is surprised to learn that no notable Latin writer of the time mentions Plutarch or his lecturing in Italy. Nor, for that matter, does Plutarch comment on the major contemporary Latin authors, such as Perseus, Lucan, Valerius Flaccus, the younger Pliny, Martial, and Quintilian. Horace is the lone exception, for he does allude to him casually, though rarely.[23] One explanation set forth (as in the essay on Plutarch in *Great Books*), namely that he was simply a provincial and thus not taken seriously by Roman authors, cannot be accepted. Later references to Plutarch abound in history since his lifetime to indicate the high regard in which he was held by learned peoples in the civilized world. Though we have no undeniable documentation to confirm the point absolutely, the most plausible approach to the dearth of Latin allusions to Plutarch remains that his personal philosophical-ethical slant did not appeal to them. Primarily neo-Platonic in its bias, his way of thinking only in small part coincided with the Stoicism so pervasive in Rome at that time. As a result, it is unlikely that his lectures would strike the avant-garde writing of Rome as particularly relevant or exciting. No other alternative yet advanced holds more compelling logic.

V *Plutarch's Humanism and His Delphic Priesthood*

The last significant turn of direction in Plutarch's career is the most illuminating in comprehending him as a man and as a writer. For, without any warning, while basking in the adulation of his Roman audiences during his second lecture tour, Plutarch returned home. Returning to conquered Greece meant that he was turning his back on the popular attention of his host Romans in exchange for humble civic responsibilities in the backwater town which Chaeronea had become.

He offered no explicit explanation for his decision. We therefore are left to contemplate the abrupt move as best we can on the basis of what can be ascertained concerning Plutarch the man. Seen in terms of his attitudes about life, his return is wholly logical and in keeping with his temperament. In Rome he had earned distinction for discussing goodness and wisdom before emperors and citizens alike; and as Plutarch saw events from his vantage point, life in general was improving. His life span ran parallel with the reigns of the pronounced phil-Hellenes Nero, Domitian,

Trajan, and Hadrian. This was a period called by historians the eve of the Second Golden Age. That being so (in Plutarch's mind, at least), it would be natural that the ethically concerned Plutarch next would seek to stimulate his own dormant Greece into ameliorating its situation as best as possible. His role upon returning, as a consequence, was to devote himself to the services of the gods and to the needs of Greek society.

What Plutarch's arrival back in Greece represented in a larger sense was the strength of his humanism, a way of looking at life using the fullest resources of man's intellect and cultural heritage. That humanism is a topic explored in Chapter 4. Meanwhile, it is not too much to claim that his entire life gave evidence of a soul-consuming humanism. In all his deeds and throughout all his writings, one discovers a faith in the dignity of man. Such a notion is seminal to all humanists. Man could improve himself if he had blueprints of correct behavior before him, Plutarch further believed. And within that correlative theory lay the source for the didactic emphasis of his art, an emphasis discernible by any reader. Our later chapters dealing with the *Lives* and the *Moralia* will examine the didactic coloration in greater detail. Also part and parcel of Plutarch's thinking process was his urgent sense of responsibility. Consequently, if we add together these determining personality characteristics and place them within a humanistic context, his rejoining his Greek compatriots becomes totally comprehensible.

To sum up, Plutarch's humanism was a unique combination of his intellect, accepting as part of its obligation toward self-cultivation and betterment the revealing of the "good life" to one's fellow men. As is evident in the *Parallel Lives,* a display of actions to be emulated (or, in certain cases to be eschewed) is possible through an examination of the heroic deeds of the past. Another more direct method would be to lead others to proper actions by making one's own life a model. In turning his attentions to improving his homeland, Plutarch proved that he would follow both routes, and that he "himself regarded public life as providing the fullest opportunity for the exercise of moral qualities." [24]

The tasks which Plutarch was to undertake back in Hellas were varied both as to function and importance. The notion of serving obviously was of utmost significance, not the trappings of any given office. Aside from serving as chief magistrate or archon in

Chaeronea, for example, he held several additional posts ranging from *agonothetes* or "Director of the Games" under Hadrian's auspices to *proedros* or chairman of the Amphictyonic Council which traditionally met at Delphi.

More representative of the truth that Plutarch "united the sacredotal with the magistratial character" (Langhorne, p. xxix) was his extended tenure as priest at Delphi. Nearly all the complex strands of Plutarch's nature, those humanistic or not, converge in holding the head position at Delphi which in no way can be considered to have been merely an honorary one. No glamor was associated with the Delphic Oracle by this time in history; diligent efforts were needed to physically sustain the temples and to maintain Apollo's shrine as reputable and worthwhile. The heyday of the Pythian prophetess was behind by then, and no self-aggrandizement was even remotely possible with that declined religious institution. Plutarch nonetheless established a second home at Delphi, twenty miles from his homestead at Chaeronea, in order to better fulfill his duties there, duties which were to last for twenty years.

As the center of Plutarch's activities for the last decades of his life, Delphi would be for him of special interest for more than one reason. Most critical of all would be what the shrine signified in Greek history as well as in everyday life during his age. Obviously the oracle was viewed as spokesman for metaphysical communications, an archetypal religious channel in the standard sense. For a learned man like him who had been extensively exposed to the growing wonders of a Roman cosmos, Delphi remained an impressive landmark in Greek history. And though, as Plutarch assumed his responsibilities there, the sanctuary may have appeared impoverished and for the most part ignored, for him the site held urgent psychological import with regard to the subjugated Hellenic spirit.

Delphi once had been supreme. Of the several temples dedicated to Apollo in which oracles answered inquiries of Hellenes and strangers alike, Delphi had enjoyed the greatest reputation during the centuries of Greece's own grandness. Starting with the gradual extension of Roman power in the third and second centuries B.C., there was less and less that could be asked the Pythia, the woman intermediary between Apollo and the utterances which then needed to be interpreted by the Delphic priest. The

Romans held no allegiance for the pronouncements at Delphi and would have no reason to consult the priest for answers either public or political in nature. Although private Roman citizens thereafter inquired concerning their personal affairs, the Roman state itself never again consulted Delphi on official business after the Second Punic War. Inasmuch as the other cities and states of Hellas had progressively less control over their own destinies, they had less occasion to call upon the oracle regarding policy matters. Simultaneously, the populations of Greece proper were dwindling, resulting in fewer personal inquiries.

All these factors combined with internal mismanagement of sacred funds, the sackings by barbarians swarming over Delphi and northern Hellas from the north, and confiscation of temple wealth by some Roman commanders, such as Sulla. The result was that by the first century B.C., Delphi ceased to function as a viable religious center.[25] Whereas three oracles were needed to respond to the heavy demands of inquirers when Apollo's cult was at its peak, the Delphic chambers remained almost abandoned by the time Plutarch accepted his priesthood in the second century A.D. In any long-range analysis of possible benefits accruing to Greece by way of Rome's rise to dominance, the fortunes of Delphi cannot be included. As scholars of the oracle have made clear, "The *Pax Romana* of the Augustan age brought no revival of fame or prosperity to Delphi. . . ." [26]

Despite what could seem depressing circumstances surrounding Delphi, Plutarch wholeheartedly accepted the challenge of involving himself with this losing proposition. His dedication in this matter reflects another facet of the humanism we have been identifying in Plutarch. Greece both early and late in its history taught the affinity of ethics and politics, those disciplines together constituting the essential basis of the true Hellenic *paideia*.[27] If the road to an ambitious career within active, dynamic politics was barred to an intelligent man like Plutarch, the equally fertile—and infinitely wide—path through ethics stood available before him. With his thorough training in humanistic doctrines, Plutarch would not have hesitated.

We already have observed that the Roman emperors immediately preceding and during Plutarch's era displayed active signs of interest in things Greek, even assisting in restoring the damaged Delphic edifice. Plutarch's precise credit in temporarily resuscitating the oracle must remain a moot point. But the presence of a man of his reputation at the shrine as its priest certainly would not have dampened any enthusiasm flickering in a Roman governor or emperor. Nero, we have learned, inaugurated a period of Imperial patronage which culminated with the avidly pro-Hellenic sponsorship of Hadrian during Plutarch's immediate lifetime. In fact, during the reprieve of Delphi under Hadrian, the oracle even resumed framing its answers in verse form, a format which had been long abandoned.[28]

Through the combination of Hadrian's liberal hand and Plutarch's diligent cultivation, the fortunes of Pythia were permitted briefly to ascend. Eventually, too, many circumstances became directed against its being sustained for long, such as the growing skepticism of the Romans and the strengthening bonds of Christian dogma. Adding to the tarnishing process of Delphi's image was the increased carping at her, which had become popular sport. Satirists like Juvenal sniped because of the trappings of superstition which to them appeared to play so integral a part in the oracle's functioning, while the more vocal Christian apologists sought to discredit any operating system of pagan metaphysics. Hence, soon after Plutarch's death, the then-remaining Apolline sanctuaries at Claros and Branchidae along with that of Delphi faded for good as their respective oracles lapsed into total silence.[29]

Thanks then at least in part to Plutarch's efforts, Delphi enjoyed a brief blossoming under the Roman sun. His religious act of piousness at Delphi was accomplished while he simultaneously was serving a more secular cause of Boeotia, since the vitality of the shrine had direct bearing on the well-being of the citizenry in the environs. How much the populace there appreciated his energies expended on behalf of Apollo's oracle is suggested by their placing an inscription dedicated to Plutarch on a stone at Delphi, an inscription which has lasted as a memorial even until today.[30]

VI *Plutarch's World View*

But there remains much more to Plutarch than his daily activities, much more which we can only derive from his writings. Just as his humanistic upbringing helped to clarify Plutarch's need to perform as priest at Delphi, it similarly illuminates his essays which are the product of a lifetime study of philosophy. For him philosophy was not an esoteric subject demanding abstinence from material phenomena on earth. Abstractions, of course, existed in the philosophic dialectic; yet even metaphysical issues were to be viewed as essential and germane to the day-by-day existence of one's life. Neither abstractions nor mundane topics, in turn, could be fully comprehended until man's knowledge, inherited or logically conceived, was brought into account. Thus the intellectual legacy of mankind, a point central to humanism of any epoch, was integral to Plutarch's philosophic scheme. In his essay on the education of youth, he elevates learning to the highest rank in human experience: "But learning, of all things in this world, is alone immortal and divine. Two elements in man's nature are supreme over all—mind and reason. The mind exercises control over reason, and reason is the servant of the mind, unassailable by fortune, impregnable to calumny, uncorrupted by disease, unimpaired by old age" ("The Education of Children," *Moralia,* I, 25).

Humanistic emphasis on the powers of the rational mind can be discerned here instantly. For Plutarch the necessary learning to develop reason derives from the study of philosophy—the best that has been thought by the human mind concerning man's context in the world. Clearly, the term "philosophy" was employed within a broader range of possibilities in his day than ours when he writes: "For through philosophy and in company with philosophy it is possible to attain knowledge of what is honourable and what is shameful, what is just and what is to be avoided, how a man must bear himself in his relation with the gods, with his parents, with his elders, with the laws, with strangers, with those in authority, with friends, with women, with children, with servants . . ." ("The Education of Children," *Moralia,* I, 35).[31]

In the chapters to follow, we shall see that all Plutarch's writings, in whatever form, are informed by his humanistic philosophy: man can behave evilly and cruelly to be sure; but man also has the capacity for laudable, glorious action. As long as that remains true for Plutarch, he will appeal to that second possibility in man by way of narratives from past history or more directly through moral axioms. In his essays Plutarch remains a man with a mission, just as was true in his personal career.

CHAPTER 2

The Lives *of Plutarch*

WHEN Plutarch returned to Chaeronea after his second combined lecture and diplomatic tour in Rome, he brought with him notes and sketches from his wide lecturing. More importantly, he came back a man who had witnessed the vigor of Roman dominion. His firsthand experiences abroad were coupled with the more universal philosophical concepts kept fresh in his mind through his lectures; together, they left him much to contemplate back in his tiny Greek home town. The remainder of Plutarch's life was to be spent serving in a series of civic and religious capacities. At the same time, he composed two significant bodies of writing, the *Moralia* and the *Parallel Lives.* Of the former we shall have occasion to speak later. For the present we shall turn to the *Lives,* praised by the classicist Gilbert Murray as "perhaps the most widely and permanently attractive work by one author known to the world."[1]

Originally, the *Parallel Lives,* which like the *Moralia* grew out of Plutarch's abundant lecture notes, numbered over fifty. Plutarch's plan was to pair notable Greeks from past history with grand Romans whose careers granted valid comparisons. Extant today are twenty-three such pairs of worthies and four single life stories. Traces remain, also, of twelve more Lives which are lost to us. Plutarch discerned sufficient details for a comparison in his sets, and he provided formal comparisons (of varying astuteness and excellence) of which eighteen remain. The traditional order of the *Lives* is as listed below:

The Traditional Order of the *Lives**

(1) Theseus and Romulus
(2) Lycurgus and Numa
(3) Solon and Publicola
(4) Themistocles and Camillus
(5) Pericles and Fabius Maximus

---

* The traditional order given above is that used in the Loeb Classical Library editions: *Plutarch's Parallel Lives,* 11 volumes (Cambridge,

(6) Alcibiades and Coriolanus
(7) Timoleon and Aemilius Paulus
(8) Pelopidas and Marcellus
(9) Aristides and Cato the Elder
(10) Philopoemen and Flamininus
(11) Pyrrhus and Caius Marius
(12) Lysander and Sulla
(13) Cimon and Lucullus
(14) Nicias and Crassus
(15) Sertorius and Eumenes
(16) Agesilaüs and Pompey
(17) Alexander and Julius Caesar
(18) Phocion and Cato the Younger
(19) Agis and Cleomenes, and Tiberius and Caius Gracchus
(20) Demosthenes and Cicero
(21) Demetrius and Antony
(22) Dion and Brutus
(23) Aratus
(24) Artaxerxes
(25) Galba
(26) Otho

I *The* Lives *as History*

The full worth of Plutarch's efforts in the *Lives* remains only partly appreciated by some readers, specifically by those who demand to know whether the *Lives* are history or biography. If one does read them as history, problems arise. Purist historians oftentimes view Plutarch as no trustworthy recorder of history. They explicitly indict Plutarch for fictionalizing and interpreting too freely the events he recites. Moreover, as stated by such a critic, Plutarch "is often being careless and inaccurate for no other reason than indifference to the kind of accuracy we prize above all in the historian." [2] The classical scholar J. P. Mahaffy considers Plutarch "garrulous," without even a redeeming agent of humor in his writings.[3] Even Bernadotte Perrin, a respected translator of his work, remarks on his "amiable weaknesses as a judge of historical evidence; his relish for the personal anecdote and the *mot;* his disregard of the logic and chronology of events; his *naïve* appropriation of the literary product of others; his consummate art in making deeds and words, whether authentic or not, portray a preconceived character. . . ." [4]

What is evident in these opinions is the traditional reluctance of the historically oriented mind to view commentaries like Plu-

---

Mass.: Harvard University Press, and London: William Heinemann Ltd., 1914–1926). Except when otherwise explicitly stated, all quotations from Plutarch's writings in this book, both from the *Lives* and the *Moralia*, will be drawn from the Loeb editions, with section or chapter numbers given first, followed by the specific page reference.

tarch's as anything except history with its concomitant evaluating criteria. Nor is the negative response to biographical narratives restricted to our age; for centuries there has existed only an uncertain acceptance of the form generally.[5] The issue at stake with respect to the *Lives* is less Plutarch's specific biographical sketches themselves than the difficulty encountered by the modern mind to catalogue those writings neatly. In previous eras history *was* biography and served an overtly ethical function. Indeed, as literary historians and critics emphasize, most writing from earlier centuries had beneath it at least alleged didactic foundations, from Horace on. Such could be expected from Western cultures weaned on the ancient dictum that letters needed both to teach and to delight. Oliver Goldsmith, to take but one example, enthusiastically espoused Plutarch's life sketches. For him and right-thinking men in the Age of Enlightenment, Plutarch's *Lives* served two critical roles aside from any strict historical illumination. In his often quoted "Preface" to the *Lives* (1762), Goldsmith spoke from and for a long tradition: "Biography has, ever since the days of *Plutarch*, been considered as the most useful manner of writing, not only from the pleasure it affords the imagination, but from the instruction it artfully and unexpectedly conveys to the understanding. It furnishes us with an opportunity of giving advice freely, and without offence." [6]

It is only when we attempt to classify biography as a branch of history that we run into an impasse. The resemblances between the two are apparent enough. Both delve into people, events, and the corresponding cultural milieus, and then both seek to interpret what is discovered. What differentiates the two fields markedly, however, is the focus. In his research into the unique genre of biography, Paul Kendall isolated the crucial distinction lucidly: "The historian frames a cosmos of happenings, in which men are included only as event-producers or event-sufferers [*sic*]. The biographer explores the cosmos of a single being." [7]

II *The* Lives *as Biography*

Not only does Plutarch operate in life sketches, not histories; he also writes in another over-all context.[8] Although biography might have commenced as an offshoot of history, it developed early along its own lines. That is a process which we cannot pursue in depth here. We can say, nonetheless, that in a rudimentary shape biography existed as far back as the sixth or seventh century B.C. with the earliest version of a Life of Homer, though the first regular biography set in a historical framework usually is considered to be Xenophon's *Agesilaus.*[9]

Plutarch consequently had a variety of precedents from which to draw when he began writing at the turn of the first Christian century—a period, incidentally, which also saw the vigorous revival of the biographical form in works by Philostratus and Tacitus in addition to that of Plutarch. Theophrastus' *Characters,* for example, furnished brief portraits of imaginary personality types; Xenophon's *Memorabilia* was comprised of episodic biographical sketches; Plato's numerous dialogues revealed character through conversations and actions; and the so-called Peripatetic biographies employed the psychological in their method, thereby bringing out personality types.[10] Nor was Plutarch lacking in straightforward historical accounts of earlier times. A prodigious reader, he gives evidence of knowing well the writings of Herodotus, Thucydides, Xenophon, Ephorus, Timaeus, Theopompus, Poseidonius, Polybius, and Strabo.[11] In hewing his way through the materials at his disposal, Plutarch formulated his own personal biographical technique wherein he openly differentiated between biography and history. Man and his character, particularly his ethical nature, were Plutarch's central concern. What we call history remained simply the backdrop against which human deeds were performed.

That he was fully aware he pursued a course not strictly historical, and thus anticipated later criticism of his approach, is best shown through his own words on the subject. In opening his commentary concerning Alexander, he pronounces his precise intentions for the *Lives* as a whole. No fair examination of Plutarch can exclude his testament:

> For it is not Histories that I am writing, but Lives; and in the most illustrious deeds there is not always a manifestation of virtue or vice, nay, a slight thing like a phrase or a jest often makes a greater revelation of character than battles where thousands fall, or the greatest armaments, or sieges of cities. Accordingly, just as painters get the likenesses in their portraits from the face and the expression of the eyes, wherein the character shows itself, but make very little account of the other parts of the body, so I must be permitted to devote myself

rather to the signs of the soul in men, and by means of these to portray the life of each, leaving to others the description of their great contests. (LCL, Vol. VII, Ch. I, 225)

Since Plutarch's methodology places less emphasis on particular political circumstances and rather more on those "signs of the soul in men," it is not surprising that his casual attitude toward concrete data has not received the seal of historical authority. In more instances than he has been given credit for, however, Plutarch followed trustworthy sources faithfully. Moreover, if we honestly take into account the multitude and variety of materials from which he drew during an age when written texts were rare and at a premium, then we must temper initial reaction to his syncretistic writing manner. Simply to say that his "sources were monumental," as does Bernadotte Perrin in her "Introduction" to *Plutarch's Themistocles and Aristides* (p. 10), scarcely reflects the task Plutarch faced to satisfy his objectives. The polite conversations of literary circles and other oral accounts had to supplement facts gleaned from his impressive reading. And when no absolutely reliable source could be located for an episode, fable, as the next best authority, had to be used.

It should be recalled that much ancient knowledge passed successfully down to us initially was promulgated orally in a tradition long since accepted without question where literature is concerned. The recitation of tales, stories, and fables from one generation to the next in certain instances was the sole means of passage for information. Plutarch was not unaware, at the same time, of the distortions, exaggerations, or omissions which may be introduced in such a process of transmission. Consequently, he began the *Life of Theseus* with a crucial comment:

May I therefore succeed in purifying Fable, making her submit to reason and take on the semblance of History. But where she obstinately disdains to make herself credible, and refuses to admit any element of probability, I shall pray for kindly readers, and such as receive with indulgence the tales of antiquity. (LCL, Vol. I, Ch. I, 5)

At least one additional matter of high importance enters any equitable consideration of the *Lives*. What inspired Plutarch to write the *Lives* and to match them as he did, and what ultimately were his projected goals in setting them down in the first place? For nearly a century, the sole full-length study in English of him was that by Archbishop Richard C. Trench of Dublin.[12] As a result, Trench's uncontested analysis of Plutarch's intentions served for decades as the definitive position. According to Trench, the pensive Plutarch, looking about him at the degraded state of Greece, was fired by a desire to speak out to the world, to declare that Hellas like Rome was capable of world-shaking actions, as Greece's glorious past had proved.[13] More specifically, Trench affirmed, Plutarch wished to call attention back to Greece and to "what manner and breed of men she once had borne, men that could be matched and paired with the best and greatest among that other people which, having passed her in the race, was now marching in the forefront of the world." [14]

Trench's opinion that Plutarch had been chauvinistically inspired became the conventional view.[15] But that standard interpretation was not totally convincing to every scholar, so that a gradually more moderate stand concerning Plutarch's aim developed. Bernadotte Perrin, to illustrate, declared that it was uncertain whether he meant to convince "reluctant Greeks that there were Romans who could well bear comparison with the greatest Greeks, or to remind the too complacent Romans" that the Greeks had attained as much as they had at one time.[16] In recent years, the moderate view has taken root which states that the *Lives* were designed to edify Greeks and Romans alike.[17]

As frequently is the case in controversies, the explicit pronouncements by the person being disputed are overlooked. Nowhere in the *Lives* or the *Moralia* does Plutarch state purely patriotic aims. When Roman and Greek personages are evaluated and compared, no consistent pattern of favoritism can be claimed. Hence, when the French classical scholar Robert Flacelière writes of the *Lives* that "It was their author's intention that each of these biographies should constitute a chapter in a study of the heroic virtues," Flacelière enjoys a firsthand authority behind him, Plutarch himself.[18] Plutarch's ethical impulse—his didactic spirit—serves as the motivating source of energy for the *Lives*. For Plutarch in classical times, as for Renaissance humanists and many intellectuals thereafter, the recounting of great men's lives was most valuable for the revelation of virtues and vices in man's nature. His own words to this effect are found at the beginning of the *Life of Timoleon:*

> I began the writing of my "Lives" for the sake of others, but I find that I am continuing the work and delighting in it now for my own sake also, using history as a mirror and endeavouring in a manner to fashion and adorn my life in conformity with the virtues therein depicted. (LCL, Vol. VI, Ch. I, 261)

Part of what some critics consider Plutarch's disinterest in temporal and political circumstances was simply a shift away from those things believed essential only in a materialistic, time-conscious world. Instead, he sought to distill the abstract and universal values found in men's lives, thereby to aid all men through the derived ethical *dicta.* That he should employ biographical writings for a morally didactic purpose is not out of the ordinary. Only in recent years has it seemed necessary to state that both good and ill deeds can provide moral enlightenment.[19] As a consequence, we need to accept Plutarch's stated means and ends regarding the nature of the *Lives.* It is ethical edification that underlies these narratives, not any subversive attempt to compensate for Greece's belabored, subordinate status in what had become a Roman cosmos.

III *A Look at the* Lives

Plutarch used no systematic approach to the events in the lives of his subjects. Certain features could be counted on for examination without question, naturally. One's talent and success in making war, for instance, rarely were omitted, because normally it was through warring that a man in the ancient world earned his fame. Aristotle and Socrates were the exception, not the rule. In many cases a man's capacities in civic affairs and reforms were treated at length. Feats of courage, or of unforgivable cowardice, were taken into account, just as were one's daily relationships with peers, superiors, and subordinates. How the protagonist nurtured his career was considered, along with his attitude toward culture and society, which helped to indicate the range of his humanity. Taken together, such varied criteria coalesced in Plutarch's sketches to form the portrait of the hero's standards, his aims, and his successes. In short, exactly as he promised, he set forth the "signs of the soul in men."

THESEUS. A book of this size cannot convey the essential facts and significances of all fifty Plutarchian Lives. Still, by our brief consideration of a selected handful, we can sample the variety of approaches he utilized in his treatment of the events and character attributes involved in a man's life record. It is interesting that Plutarch bypassed figures like the legendary Heracles (or Hercules), whose stature as the strongest mortal had granted him universal renown in all ages. Feats of limitless strength alone did not qualify a man for his literary pantheon. The intellect held a central position in his appraisals along with physical achievements, even if the superior mind concerned developed craft and cunning for evil ends.[20] Theseus epitomizes those heroes chosen by Plutarch who excelled both in the arena of armed might and in imaginative civil innovations. Like so many other protagonists in literature, Theseus at first was raised as an unknown child, though princely born as son of Aegeus. His name, plausibly derived from the Greek noun "place," implied that he had been placed in a spot where he could be found by allegedly surrogate parents who would raise the child until a propitious moment. In the case of Theseus, his mother Aethra and his grandfather Pittheus cared for the boy but kept his true birth from him. Then, in perfect accordance with traditional rites of passage, the young man set off on a journey (in this instance to Athens) to locate his royal father and reclaim his true identity.

Plutarch makes it clear that Theseus was no average lad by emphasizing his unflinching courage, a definite reflection of his spirit and soul. Instead of traveling by sea to Athens, Theseus ignored his mother's instructions and, instead, struck out by land through territories infested with murderous brigands. As Plutarch explains, Theseus was eager to pursue the more perilous option because he had been fired by "the valour of Heracles, until by night his dreams were of the hero's achievements, and by day his ardour led him along and spurred him on in his purpose to achieve the like" (VI, 15–17). As is quickly established by his remarks, Plutarch was interested only indirectly in an archetypal warrior such as Heracles, as a model fighter whose physical prowess inspired the more complete hero who possesses intelligence as well as brawn.

Plutarch's narrative moves swiftly as he tells of Theseus' arrival in Athens. Theseus kept his identity secret until he could show Aegeus the unique sword and other tokens of his birth; only then was the son confirmed to the happy father. After he had put down a treacherous uprising by the sons of Pallas, Theseus was left with little to do, a situation, Plutarch explains, anathema to the adventurous spirit of the youth. Desiring a task and further approval of the Athenians, Theseus undertakes another perilous feat by going out to fight the Marathonian bull which had been threatening the city.

Even more impressive conquests lay ahead of the heir to Athens' throne. Most often Theseus' name is heard in connection with the Minotaur and Labyrinth of Crete. In keeping with Plutarch's regular procedure when several versions of the same tale are extant, he covers them all in his accounts. Minos had been harassing Athens for years, demanding an extraordinary tribute for Crete of seven boys and seven girls. Theseus, gloriously confident, demanded to be sent to Crete as part of that tribute. Once in Crete, he received from Ariadne (who loved him) the golden thread which would permit him to find his way through the intricate design of the Labyrinth. Once safely outside the maze, he killed the Minotaur and sailed off with Ariadne and the freed hostages. Plutarch at this point offers two variations of the same episode. One tells of Theseus defeating the mighty Taurus in single combat to win the love of Ariadne and the admiration of her father Minos, who promptly frees all Athenian hostages on the island. The second variation speaks of the hero secretly sailing to Crete where he overpowers enemy forces and attains a nonwar pact between Athens and Crete.

Along with Theseus' shrewd ability came culpability, for not everything Plutarch reports about his protagonist is complimentary. In one episode during the return home aboard ship, Ariadne, pregnant with Theseus' child, was forced to debark on an island because of extreme labor discomforts. Because of Theseus' carelessness, the ship sailed away without her, leaving the agonized woman to die alone. Additionally, when his ship finally approached the coast near Attica, the overly elated Theseus forgot to mount the flag denoting safe passage. King Aegeus, grief-stricken upon seeing the forgotten pennant of doom flying from the mast of his son's ship, threw himself down the rocks to his death. Also,

Plutarch objectively reports Theseus' misconduct with women. Besides marrying four or five women—and abandoning them for still others—Theseus ravished many more, including the renowned Helen. This last deed brought war to Attica and eventually banishment and death to Theseus. What becomes clear in these commentaries is that even when he greatly admired his hero subject, Plutarch gave a full, honest rendering of conduct.

It was in governmental innovations that Theseus excelled, Plutarch believed. After Aegeus' death, for example, it was Theseus' notion to unite the separate communities and townships of Attica into a single entity, the one proposal for which he is best known. Once he had assured the separate units that each would be considered equal to the other, the union took place, thus creating the formal Athens still remaining. In addition, Theseus had new money coined and stamped with Athens' unique seal; he set famous pillars (as on the Isthmus between Ionia and Peloponnesus); he instituted the Isthmian games in honor of Poseidon; and he waged a campaign against the Amazons, taking captive their queen Hippolyta (or Antiope, according to another version Plutarch acknowledges).

Despite his positive achievements, Theseus was plagued by his rash deeds, such as the rape of Helen. And the difficulties which thereupon ensued were to lead to his final destruction. Plutarch recounts the details fully, underscoring the irony in the manner of Theseus' death. After failing to recapture leadership of Athens, which had rebuffed him for his general misconduct, Theseus lived in exile on the island of Scyros. But the jealous island king, Lycomedes, by treacherous means threw Theseus over the cliffs to a death remarkably parallel to his father's. Only later, Plutarch makes clear, did Athens forgive its founder and satisfy the Oracle of Delphi by returning Theseus' bones to the city for a final honorable interment.

ROMULUS. Quite reasonably, Plutarch juxtaposes the commentary on Theseus' life with that of Romulus. At the outset of the narrative treating Theseus, Plutarch explained the basis for the match: ". . . it seemed to me that I must make the founder of lovely and famous Athens the counterpart and parallel to the father of invincible and glorious Rome" (I,5). Plutarch further maintained that both protagonists were of "uncertain and obscure parentage," that both "got the reputation of descent from gods," and that thanks to their respective combinations of strength and wisdom, each made genuine metropolises of their cities.

A lesser chronicler well might have given up in despair about the origins of Rome and its alleged founder Romulus. But Plutarch gamely accepted the challenge and began his account of Romulus by considering the source of the name Rome. Reflecting sound research on the subject, he recited the myriad possible sources: in the *Aeneid*, the woman who urged that the boats be burned was called Roma, and because her advice was taken, the peoples had to settle there; Roma also was the name of the daughter of Italus and Leucaria; Romanus, son of Odysseus and Circe, supposedly colonized the city; Romis was the tyrant of the Latins, and so on. Thus the reader early is exposed to Plutarch's love of etymology. The fact emerges that, frequently in his writing, he muses in this fashion about word origins and derivations.

In the version of Rome's founding most favored by Plutarch, the archetypal pattern involved is that of Cain and Abel. Two competing brothers, Amulius and Numitor, contested the throne of the city Alba, until Amulius, the more powerful, finally seized control. By Mars, giant and wondrous twin sons were born to Numitor's daughter Ilia (or Rhea or Silvia, the exact name remaining uncertain). The wary Amulius, fearing the birth of such twins, commanded his servant to do away with the babes by leaving them on the river bank. Fable then had it that there, near a fig tree, the boys were preserved and suckled by a wolf, giving rise to the bestknown theory concerning the names of the twins and ultimately that of Rome. In Plutarch's words: "Moreover, we are told that they were named, from 'ruma,' the Latin word for *teat*, Romulus and Romus (or Remus), because they were seen sucking the wild beast" (VI, 103). Taking charge of the abandoned babies were Faustulus, a swineherd of Amulius, and his wife, states Plutarch. When the youths were sufficiently grown, Numitor drew them into a revolt against the hated Amulius, and for Romulus a life of violence began. With Romulus attacking from without the city and Romus from within, Amulius soon was defeated. An argument between the brothers then ensued regarding the establishment of a new city, and through trickery Romulus slew Romus. Romulus then laid out a city in a circular pattern, plowed a trench for the boundary, and had the historic walls built. The founding date for what was to become Rome, Plutarch informs us, generally is assumed to be April 21 in about 754 B.C.[21]

Equally central to Romulus' life was the infamous "Rape of the Sabines." For the most part, emphasizes Plutarch, Romulus was revered by foreigners. But one particular antagonism, that between the Romans and the Sabines, persisted. Concerning the long-standing feud, Plutarch wholly discounted Livy's account. Instead, Plutarch held that during special religious games and upon a signal from Romulus, his men seized and raped hundreds of Sabine maidens. Married women were left untouched, except for one sole error which Plutarch documents faithfully. Such a deed, insists Plutarch, was not done out of lust, "but with the fixed purpose of uniting and blending the two peoples in the strongest bonds" (XIV, 131). Eventually the stratagem worked. A truce was arranged wherein the Sabines and Romans merged, adopting and learning each other's ways.

Although still admired by some, Romulus seemed to change after his final battle against the Tuscans. He became more haughty, arrogant, and autocratic, until the general populace were disenchanted with him. Soon thereafter the masses were joined by the patricians who similarly grew to disapprove of Romulus, in their case because of certain rulings he made injurious to their cause. Without any warning, after he had ruled Rome for thirty-eight years, Romulus vanished during a storm while outdoors in a public gathering. Plutarch carefully adds a polemical epilogue to the episode which strongly implies that the angered patricians had murdered Romulus during the blinding storm. They then foisted on the dazed citizens the tale of Romulus' godlike ascension into heaven. Here, as elsewhere, Plutarch enters his view strictly as a personal opinion. Nearly always in such instances, he makes known that what he presents is simply a probability, not a historically affirmable fact.

The formal comparison Plutarch furnishes for the lives of Theseus and Romulus probably is his most profound. In it he reveals a fundamentally naturalistic view of man, insofar as man's habits, cultivated over years, are mixed with his fortune to determine his fate. At the same time, a man's unique, individual personality with its proclivities for both evil and good also bears urgently on one's life. Plutarch's position, quasiexistential as it appears to be here, finds man defining himself. Man, insists Plutarch, must be held accountable for his acts:

Again, if the misfortunes of men are not to be attributed altogether to fortune, but to the different habits and passions which will be found underlying them, then no one shall acquit Romulus of unreasoning anger or hasty and senseless wrath in dealing with his brother, nor Theseus in dealing with his son, although the cause which stirred his anger leads us to be more lenient towards the one who was overthrown by a stronger provocation, as by a heavier blow. (III, 193)

Plutarch astutely observes the differences in motivations behind the actions of his heroes, preferring Theseus on this count because he acted of his own accord to reach for great achievements, whereas Romulus "proceeded to perform great exploits under compulsion" (I, 189). On the other hand, when actual accomplishments are weighed by Plutarch, the fact that Romulus created a world-famous city beginning with nothing was more impressive than Theseus' feat of amalgamating several smaller towns into one. Neither protagonist, however, satisfied Plutarch as a monarch, because each had failed in a different manner: "Although Theseus and Romulus were both statesmen by nature, neither maintained to the end the true character of a king, but both deviated from it and underwent a change, the former in the direction of democracy, the latter in the direction of tyranny . . ." (II, 191–93). Clearly, Plutarch was concerned primarily in how successful and humane each hero was in his time. For Plutarch, his subjects remained very much alive. The passage of time could not eradicate the indelible pattern of the unique temperament of each. Plutarch's evaluating criteria, from first to last, remain those of a humanist.

LYCURGUS. Plutarch remained equitable with his heroes though they may have employed markedly different methods to reach their respective ends. A perfect illustration of that fact exists in his treatment of the lives of Lycurgus, from Sparta of the eighth century B.C., and Numa, from Rome of about the seventh century B.C. His first subject, Lycurgus, was a great favorite of Plutarch because of his supreme self-discipline, a mastery of self which Lycurgus passed on to the Spartans and which still informs our concept today of "the Spartan life" as one disavowing self-indulgence.

Originally second in line for the throne of Sparta after his older brother Polydectes, Lycurgus accepted rule only reluctantly. So desirous, in fact, was Lycurgus of appearing uninterested in assuming leadership for himself that he stayed away from governmental politicking altogether at first, traveling instead to Crete, Asia, and Egypt. While distant from Sparta and preceding his rule, Lycurgus made good use of his journeys. As Plutarch elaborates the case, Lycurgus learned and transmitted the cultures and mores of peoples he encountered abroad. But eventually he responded to an urgent call for administrative assistance from the Lacedaemonians, who were afflicted by internal strife. The man called by the Oracle of Delphi "beloved of the gods, and rather god than man" thereupon returned to Hellas. His first act was immediately to institute reforms requested of him to "change the existing order of things and revolutionize the civil polity" (V, 217). Specifically, he inaugurated a senate, or "Council of Elders," whose vote, in addition to that of the king, would be required to sanction policies. A second bold measure was to redistribute the land, thereby to set right basic inequalities. Further, he removed all gold and silver money from the market and replaced it with iron coin, a strong monetary measure meant to discourage dishonesty.

Because Lycurgus believed too many luxuries enervated the will of the people, he sought to discourage the accumulation of material wealth. One result was his banishment of all unnecessary and superfluous arts, including foreign wares and ornamental objects purchased for purposes of prestige. Plutarch agreed with Lycurgus' scheme, emphasizing that artisans thus were freed from useless tasks and subsequently could turn their energies to beauty and workmanship within more mundane but utilitarian articles. Nor could the wealthy indulge themselves with special foods; Lycurgus instituted common messes. Even marriages and births were closely regulated by the state, in the scheme of Lycurgus. Marriage was encouraged in many ways; bachelors were derided, for example, and girls kept scantily clad. At the same time, jealousy on behalf of one's wife or children was frowned upon. Polygamy was accepted, and marriages were consummated only at night in the dark, the sole time husband and wife had together alone. Children produced were not raised within a paternalistic family arrangement. Very early in the lives of young babies they were taken by the state which examined them carefully for health and vigor. Those children adjudged sickly and weak were left to perish in the mountains, a conventional policy in antiquity for disposing of undesirables. For Plutarch, Lycurgus' social engineering was intelligent and humane, because such close controls on human behavior permitted optimum cultivation of social relationships.

Obedience was the hallmark of Spartan education and of training for those children deemed strong enough to be taken in by the state. Seven-year-old boys were gathered into martial-like companies to be raised. Paradoxically, Lycurgus, who declared that education was "the greatest and noblest task of the law-giver" (XIV, 245), allowed only sufficient reading and writing for the elemental requirements of the youth. Instead, they were indoctrinated in a militaristic manner to "obey commands well, endure hardships, and conquer in battle" (XVI, 257). Lest his readers receive too much of a one-sided perspective of Spartan life, Plutarch at this point in his accounts inserts the balancing information that the youth also were trained in music and poetry, so that they were "thus shown to be at the same time most musical and most warlike" (XXI, 273).

On the basis of these and other remarks, it is clear Plutarch appreciated the civil polity Lycurgus designed for his people. The giving of one's self on behalf of the whole community had been an essential keystone in Plutarch's personal attitudes, as we already have seen. He felt therefore a kinship with Lycurgus, who dedicated all his people's energies to the greater common welfare. In the blueprints of that self-effacing ruler, there was no room for self-aggrandizement, a fact which Plutarch lauds in these words: "In a word, he trained his fellow-citizens to have neither the wish nor the ability to live for themselves; but like bees they were to make themselves always integral parts of the whole community, clustering together about their leaders, almost beside themselves with enthusiasm and noble ambition, and to belong wholly to their country" (XXV, 283). In light of today's apprehension of countries being overcontrolled by central governments, such sentiments as Plutarch's appear antithetical to our concepts of individual rights. But in Plutarch's era, the construction of a firm societal and political unit was viewed as meritorious. Sparta, after all, had enjoyed the highest reputation among the ancients for good government in all Hellas. Moreover, Plutarch reminds his readers, Lycurgus' laws served the people for five hundred years "in which no one of the fourteen kings who followed him made any change, down to Agis the son of Archidamus" (XXIX, 297).

NUMA. The Roman leader Numa achieved civil harmony as well, but through quite different means. After Romulus' sudden disappearance, Rome was beset by opposing factions seeking leadership. Considerable agitation continued, reports Plutarch, until the contending groups agreed to a plan whereby each side would choose a king from the ranks of the other. To Plutarch, with his humanistic instincts, the choice of Numa Pompilius from the Sabines was sound. Numa's principal attributes, declares Plutarch, derive from his having "put away from himself not only the infamous passions of the soul, but also that violence and rapacity which are in such high repute among Barbarians, believing that true bravery consisted in the subjugation of one's passions by reason" (III, 315).

Like Lycurgus, Numa at first declined the offer to rule. He was apprehensive about the arrangement because the Romans by then had become hardened into a war-oriented society and had cultivated a hunger for civil growth by conquest. Eventually, however, Numa agreed to serve, stating that his prime interest was to unite the citizens of the adjoining towns and thus halt the continuing fraternal agitation. Numa's approach to secure and maintain peace in the city was strikingly different from that of Lycurgus in Sparta. Rather than elevating the militaristic spirit, Numa waged a calculated campaign to modify the brutal, war-mongering character of the Roman people. To accomplish his aim, Numa first disbanded the personal army which Romulus previously had formed, ostensibly as a bodyguard force. At the same time, Numa openly encouraged the practice of religion in Roman life. This he did by adding to the number of priests in the city, by establishing the Pontifex Maximus as mentor of the Vestal Virgins, by instituting codified burial and mourning rites, and by setting up special priesthoods to help keep community peace through parley and discussion. Numa, in brief, sought to elicit the more domestic facets of the Roman character, while simultaneously modifying the abrasive martial inclinations.

Gradually Numa's reforms had their desired effect, because he had offered Rome alternatives to war. From the Regia, the royal house he had built, Numa carried out many sacred functions himself, officiating at sacrifices, processions, and religious dances. These activities provided the people with charming diversions that earned the favor of the masses and calmed their warlike temperaments, explains Plutarch. Furthermore, in his own life Numa incarnated the peacefulness he taught. In light of the ordinary debaucheries of so many Roman leaders, Numa's reign stood out as a rarity. Plutarch acknowledges the dimensions of Numa's achievement this way: "For there is no record either of war, or faction, or political revolution while Numa was king. Nay more, no hatred or jealousy was felt towards his person, nor did ambition lead men to plot and conspire against his throne" (XX,373). As befitted such a successful reign, Plutarch continues, Numa lived on into his eighties when he died of old age, a peaceful end to a peaceful life.

If the comparison of Theseus and Romulus earlier considered was illustrative of Plutarch at his best, then we can assume the joint evaluation of Lycurgus and Numa to be among his weakest. On the basis of his own narratives, Plutarch in this comparative section strikes many readers as arbitrary, perhaps even capricious. It is not that the entirety of his assessments are wrong-headed. Plutarch, it should be admitted, did point up the significant likenesses of the two protagonists. For example, they both revealed thoughtful moderation, piety, and talent for governing and swaying their respective peoples. Both succeeded in leading their communities to self-control and sobriety of spirit. Despite these fair observations, Plutarch abruptly expresses his own preference for Lycurgus on what appear to be tenuous grounds, namely, Lycurgus' rigid educational policies. Plutarch's rationale raises unanswered questions concerning his own concept of the family unit. Specifically, he says: "But surely, by his careful attention to boys, by their collection into companies, their discipline and constant association, and by his painstaking arrangements for their meals and bodily exercise and sports, Lycurgus proves that Numa was no more than an ordinary lawgiver. For Numa left the bringing up of youths to the wishes or necessities of their fathers" (IV,397). Criticisms of Numa no doubt could be found. But from his own accounts of Numa's life, Plutarch created a figure almost ideal as a ruler. The incongruities in Plutarch's ultimate judgment then can be attributed only to his didactic zeal. For Plutarch there remained something even more valuable than civil harmony or popularity of a regime. That something was the requisite inculcation of self-control, a seminal achievement in the disciplined society evolved under Lycurgus.

DEMOSTHENES. In his discussions of Demosthenes and Cicero, two of the most notable orators ever known, Plutarch discreetly disavows any intent to compare either their speeches or their speaking styles. His prime interest remains rooted in the soul of his subject, not in any single talent or technique. It is the pattern of the lives of the two speakers that catches Plutarch's attention first. He avers that the two men further resembled each other in "their love of distinction, their love of freedom in their political activities, and their lack of courage for wars and dangers" (III,7). Rather early and bluntly, then, Plutarch sets apart these two orators from the conventional brave heroes one expects in the realm of famed men.

As the son of a well-to-do factory owner, Demosthenes, it might have been assumed, would have had easy access to the better sort of education available for wealthy families in Greece in the fourth century B.C. But his father died when Demosthenes was only seven, with the result that wrongdoing guardians confiscated the lad's inheritance and left him in a sorry plight. His physical state was little better, writes Plutarch, because from the first he was sickly and was not allowed to partake in outdoor activities or strenuous labor. Demosthenes' relationship with other children consequently was strained, and he became the butt of many cruel jokes. Plutarch projects into the future at this point, in a foreshadowing fashion, to suggest that the early deficits in Demosthenes' life ultimately would be transformed into advantages. Indeed the upward turn in his life began the day the misfit youth heard Callistratus, the orator, argue and win a case in court. The resulting extravagant admiration shown Callistratus excited Demosthenes, who became fired to pursue a like career as orator. Not only had the praise for the speaker affected the lad, but also the power of rhetoric which could put down mighty opposition. That blossoming ambition in turn led to a rigorous regimen in his life. Plutarch describes the process, "Wherefore, bidding farewell to his other studies and to the usual pursuits of boyhood, he practised himself laboriously in declamation, with the idea that he too was to be an orator" (V,13).

Several teachers are suggested by Plutarch as having aided Demosthenes in the art of speaking, including Isaeus, Plato, and Callias the Syracusan, though no single mentor is pointed out as predominant. When he came of age, Demosthenes had cultivated a debating skill sufficient to bring suits against his former guardians. Hence something had been salvaged after all from a seemingly unfortunate early life, Plutarch emphasizes, because, "Demosthenes, after applying himself to oratory in the first place for the sake of recovering his private property, by this means acquired ability and power in speaking, and at last in public business, as it were in the great games, won the first place among the citizens who strove with one another on the bema" (VI,15). Other means, as well, by which Demosthenes cultivated his speech are recited by Plutarch, including the sound advice that Satyrus, the actor, gave him about improving the delivery of words. Also, a popular complaint concerning Demosthenes' speaking was his lisping, especially an inability to pronounce the letter "r." That fault he corrected by putting pebbles in his mouth and then reciting speeches. That remedy ever since has been firmly associated with Demosthenes' fame. Plutarch makes it clear that Demosthenes earned his renown as a great orator through diligent practice and work. To exercise his voice, for instance, Demosthenes recited aloud while running up steep hills or repeated speeches at a single breath. And as for the necessary gesticulations in the public speaking trade, Demosthenes rehearsed before a large mirror which he had propped up in his house.

At the age of thirty-two, Demosthenes commenced his public career in earnest. Though he did not enjoy a reputation in city affairs at the time, he nonetheless prepared to prosecute Meidias, a well-known citizen of great wealth also notorious for his swindling. By his very audacity in challenging such a public figure, Demosthenes instantly earned a fame for himself. The case, however, never was heard, because the young advocate reluctantly accepted three thousand drachmas from Meidias and dropped the matter. Some citizens thereupon suggested that Demosthenes had been bribed, a charge that Plutarch relates openly, as was his policy. Yet, Plutarch personally thought otherwise. Here, as we have noted several times before, Plutarch enters the historical fray when he considers the issues to be urgent. In this instance, speaking for himself, he theorizes that no amount of money could have bought off Demosthenes if the orator had believed there was any genuine chance at all of winning against Meidias' powerful defenders. Seen in other terms, Plutarch seemingly argues for the pragmatic position that discretion on Demosthenes' part was the better part of valor. However, later Plutarch proves that in this early instance he sincerely believes Demosthenes innocent, because when he finds the speaker culpable, Plutarch states that view forthrightly, as well.

Less open to debate was Demosthenes' verbal defense of the Greeks against the ambitions of Philip. In his frequent exhortations on that matter, Demosthenes earned a firm reputation and admiration throughout Greece. Once his position regarding public polity was established, Demosthenes remained faithful to it, emphasizes Plutarch, regardless of what rumors in history might have stated. Plutarch helpfully elaborates on the methods used by his protagonist: "The political attitude of Demosthenes was manifest even while peace still lasted, for he would let no act of the Macedonian pass uncensured, but on every occasion kept rousing and inflaming the Athenians against him [i.e., Philip]" (XVI, 39). Finally, when matters had reached a head, Demosthenes laid out a workable plan of action to repel Philip and the Macedonian juggernaut. The orator's pronouncements had their desired effect to rally the Greeks, who thereupon began to league themselves for battle. A tentative alliance of most of the Greek states was thus brought about.

Demosthenes' feats at this significant juncture in Greek history established him as a profoundly important figure, once and for all. He alone stepped forward to urge the Greeks to support Thebes, the sole important Greek state that did not join in the battle alliance. He traveled to Thebes to win Theban support against Philip, though it meant arguing his case in front of enemy emissaries from Philip, who were also there to receive the cooperation of the Thebans. As Plutarch recounts the crucial encounter, despite Theban terror at the impending confrontation of powers being amassed and despite the fact their own interest probably would have been better served by rejecting the Athenian pleas, the Thebans nonetheless fell beneath the spell of Demosthenes' arguments. The biographer summarizes the phenomenon this way:

> the power of the orator . . . fanned up their courage and inflamed their honourable ambition and obscured all other considerations, so that, casting away fear and calculation and feelings of obligation, they were rapt away by his words into the path of honour. And so great and glorious was the orator's success seen to be that Philip at once sent an embassy and asked for peace. (XVIII, 43–45)

At the same time, there was another less attractive facet in Demosthenes' character, one that Plutarch takes into full account. When no finite peace could be agreed upon, open conflict commenced between the Greeks and Philip's forces; and in these early skirmishes Demosthenes showed up well as a fighter. At the battle at Chaeronea in 338 B.C., however, in a moment of fright Demosthenes abandoned his post, threw down his arms, and fled most ignobly. Despite the harsh railings of politicians opposed to him, the Athenians still absolved Demosthenes of any crime in the infamous deed, and the citizens welcomed him back as a leading man of affairs. For a while, Athenian faith seemed justified, when soon afterward Philip was assassinated, causing jubilation among the Greeks. "Margites," or "silly madman" (the Greek name for Alexander, Philip's son and successor), on the other hand, swiftly settled worrisome affairs in his homeland. Thereupon he marched his forces into Boeotia where he crumpled all Athenian resistance. Instantly, Demosthenes lost both his confidence and his general support. One immediate result was that the Thebans, abandoned by their pledged allies, were forced to fight the Macedonians alone, eventually losing their city. Several times thereafter, Demosthenes went to Alexander as emissary to plead for peace. But in each instance he faltered and turned back out of fear.

The career of the orator became still more besmirched later, reveals Plutarch. With full particulars, Plutarch recounts how Harpalus, Alexander's thieving treasurer, ran off to the Athenians after having been discovered misusing state funds. Once in Athens, Harpalus found Demosthenes amenable to bribery, a fact here not disputed by Plutarch. Once the facts of his treachery were discovered, Demosthenes came under heavy attack for capitulating to gold. After a full-dress hearing before the Areiopagus, the highest council of the city, the statesman was found guilty of accepting the bribe, was fined, and then was jailed for default of the fine. Rather than abide with such a blotched reputation in Athens, he ran off to Aegina and Troezen where he lived in exile.

When Alexander died, however, the Greek state revived its demands for union and for freedom from Macedonian domination. By taking up again the rallying cry of Athenian release from its oppressors, Demosthenes won a reprieve from Athens. Soon he was welcomed back warmly from his exile, with the city dignitaries coming out to greet him. But here again, Plutarch underscores that the word does not always win out over the sword. The Attic coalition Demosthenes had helped to piece together was cursorily squelched by various new leaders of the Macedonians. When the crucial battles were lost, Demosthenes secretly fled Athens, thereby earning the death penalty as a traitor. He resided at the temple of Poseidon at Calauria where, scorning honest efforts by friends to exonerate him in Athens, he claimed his own life by taking poison.

Plutarch insists that the Athenians never were to bear a grudge against their greatest orator and one-time leader. Shortly after his death, they paid him honor by erecting a bronze statue. Plutarch rounds out his thorough commentary by citing an appropriate penetrating epitaph dedicated by the Athenians, a statement which takes into account both his brilliance and his flaw:

> If thy strength had only been equal to thy purposes, Demosthenes,
> Never would the Greeks have been ruled by a Macedonian Ares.
> (XXX, 77)

CICERO. Cicero is the natural counterpart to Demosthenes in several respects, but principally because both excelled as speakers and both were called upon (and frequently ignored) by their respective states for advice and leadership. Cicero's rise to prominence was swift and certain, writes Plutarch. He early showed sharp intelligence in his schooling, along with a talent for poetry. Through his associations with academicians (especially Greek mentors, Plutarch emphasizes), Cicero learned about law and won his first case defending the actor Roscius. But because he feared the machinations of the leader Sulla, Cicero avoided Rome, traveling instead in Greece ostensibly to improve his health, his knowledge of philosophy, and his craft of public speaking.

Before returning to Rome and the political arena upon Sulla's death in 78 B.C., Cicero first took additional time in Asia to polish himself into an even more effective orator. He was a serious learner of the art of speaking, studying with Xenocles of Adramyttium, Dionysius of Magnesia, and Menippus, according to Plutarch. In Rhodes he continued to study under Apollonius who, upon hearing Cicero declaim in Greek, lamented that even the Greek art of oratory had passed on to the Romans. Moreover, Cicero learned philosophy from Poseidonius in Rhodes, and, like Demosthenes, he perfected his speech delivery by scrutinizing the techniques used by actors.

Plutarch takes care to assemble these details of Cicero's training to suggest to his readers that diligent exploitation of one's mental abilities also can lead to renown and power as can sheer might. In the case of Cicero, as with Demosthenes, the careful preparatory grooming paid off. Thanks in part to his adeptness in communicating orally with the people, Cicero in his early posts of leadership established a reputation for honesty and fairness. Indeed, his advance in Roman political affairs progressed smoothly in general, with ever higher positions assigned him. At the same time, Cicero's rising popularity did not lead to his becoming careless about the pitfalls which await an aspiring and successful statesman. With fascinating details, Plutarch recounts the infamous treacheries of Catiline against Cicero and the Roman Senate. Cicero remained alert, however, and parried every intrigue initiated by Catiline and his conspirators. Moreover, Plutarch points out that Cicero earned still fuller admiration from his noble peers by having disposed of Catiline's schemes in a quiet fashion, thereby avoiding the spread of needless alarm and tension among the masses.

To be sure, Cicero had jealous detractors, and paralleling his growth in influence was the increase in numbers of enemies. All the same, indicates Plutarch, some of the friction was deserved. With complete candor, Plutarch elaborates on the character trait that became most injurious to Cicero's fame and that made him vulnerable to opponents. Of greatest significance was his indiscretion in what he said, a problem doubly hazardous for Cicero who was inclined to gossip excessively. Thus, paradoxically, the verbal agility which helped elevate Cicero to a position of honor and importance in Rome also was to assist in the deterioration of his reputation. Plutarch expands on the situation. First, he explains, although Cicero liberally appreciated the deeds of others and offered credit when it was due, he also was free in bragging about himself. The irony of noble Cicero cheapening his greatness through such a petty flaw was not lost on Plutarch, who reports: "So at this time Cicero had the greatest power in the state, but he made himself generally odious, not by any base action, but by continually praising and magnifying himself, which made him hateful to many" (XXIV, 141). In addition, Cicero harmed his cause irreparably among Roman colleagues through his caustic, satiric humor. A rich tableau of daily Roman society comes to life for the reader as Plutarch enumerates explicit instances of Cicero's indelicate gibes. For example, Cicero insisted on using an insulting nickname for Marcus Aquinius, he made open fun of Lucius Cotta's drinking excesses, he bluntly described how ugly Voconius' daughter was, he teased Marcus Gellius about his possible servile birth, and he ridiculed Sulla's son, Faustus, to his face concerning his notorious prodigality. Plutarch impresses upon his readers that Cicero lost needed popular support by his thoughtless pronouncements. Jesting taunts have a legitimate place against political and legal opponents, concludes Plutarch; but indiscriminate verbal attacks, simply for laughs, only cause hatred.

Notwithstanding his personal disappointment in a man like Cicero who was not in full control of himself, Plutarch provides his readers with a balanced account of his hero. In part, suggests Plutarch, Cicero's career was inhibited by his thoughtless talk which earned him the animosity of other Roman legislators, influential men whose aid Cicero later would need. But equally unfortunate for Cicero were the historical circumstances of his time, which first pitted Julius Caesar against Pompey for rule of Rome, and then led to a fierce power struggle among Caesar's assassins. In the first matter, Cicero made a noble effort to reconcile Pompey and Caesar in hopes thereby of retaining the senate form of rule in Rome. At that very time, however, Caesar crossed the Rubicon, so alarming Pompey that he fled. After first siding with Pompey briefly, Cicero had second thoughts about the dispute and went over to Caesar. And once Caesar took firm control of Rome, Cicero abstained from all public affairs, affirms Plutarch. Instead, he turned to teaching philosophy to the young elite of the city. But his secure situation out of political warfare ended abruptly when Julius Caesar suddenly was slain. Cicero then was subjected to strong counterpressures from the new contenders for Caesar's power, each of whom sought the endorsement of the celebrated and influential orator-statesman. Cicero eventually threw his support in the senate behind young Octavius Caesar and thereby assured his own doom when Octavius proved no less mercenary than the others. Cicero's last official act, well-intentioned though it was, lost Rome what remaining strength it had barely managed to keep under Julius Caesar's revived dictatorship previously. Plutarch's commentary at this point mirrors both his personal disappointment at events and Cicero's bitter frustration: "For this he was blamed by his friends at the time, and shortly afterwards he perceived that he had ruined himself and betrayed the liberty of the people" (XLVI, 201).

Happily for his readers, Plutarch does not draw out the resultant assassination of Cicero. The end came on December 7, 43 B.C., Plutarch reports, when Cicero was sixty-four years old. His head and hands were lopped off and presented to Antony, who expressed great elation upon their receipt. Roman citizens, however, shuddered at these actions. Plutarch's theory that fortunes do not remain constant is validated here, when he projects his accounts into the future beyond Cicero's slaying to tell of Antony's eventual defeat at the hands of the younger Caesar a dozen years later. He ironically underscores the fact that Antony's name at the later moment in history was stripped of all honors, while Cicero's son was established as Caesar's colleague in office.

Plutarch's comparisons of Demosthenes and Cicero earn our respect for their acuity. No taint of prejudice on behalf of the Greek hero can be suggested here either, as might have been the case with Lycurgus and Numa. The assessments strike us as wholly fair. Demosthenes, on the one hand, had "no prettiness or pleasantry," while Cicero often was carried away by his love of jest. And whereas Demosthenes said little in self-praise, Cicero's excessive boasting, Plutarch claims, gave evidence of an immoderate hunger for fame. Nonetheless, with respect to the ultimate welfare of the state, he clearly endorses Cicero's behavior: "And surely in the matter of banishment, at least, for the one it was disgraceful, since he had been convicted of theft; but for the other it was a most honourable result, since he had rid his country of baleful men" (IV, 219).

CHAPTER 3

Alexander and Caesar: Two Giants in the Lives

I *Exceptional Specimens of Plutarch's Craft*

AMONG the best balanced and most satisfying of the biographies are those of Alexander and Caesar. The countless exciting episodes in the lifetime of each guaranteed keenly interested reading audiences for Plutarch's commentaries in every subsequent age. Both Caesar and Alexander, to illustrate, provided Plutarch with Gargantuan historical figures who cast mammoth shadows across the horizons of their eras. In addition, to an astonishing degree they carved out their own destinies through their actions and then were cut off prematurely by the very events they had helped to set in motion. The drama inherent in the lives of the two was so tellingly conveyed in Plutarch's portraits that many centuries later literary artists like Shakespeare were to be ignited by the same heat that fired Plutarch originally.

ALEXANDER. As Plutarch offers us the story of Alexander, we are meant to sense his mysterious charisma. His parents, both Philip and Olympias, experienced dreams that their offspring would be a unique, outstanding figure. Olympias, Plutarch reveals, dreamed of a thunderbolt in her womb the night before her marriage, and Philip after the wedding had visions of having placed a seal with the shape of a lion on his wife's womb. In addition, as was Plutarch's custom, the biographer repeats associated but unverified stories, such as one intimating that Alexander actually had been conceived by Olympias with the aid of a god, an apocryphal device commonly related to the birth of an exceptional man in antiquity. Whatever the exact circumstances, Plutarch goes on to state that Alexander was born in July of 356 B.C., with numerous auspicious omens commemorating the event.

After commenting on the specialness of Alexander's birth, he speeds his narrative, foregoing all the usual details regarding the lad's early years. But what Plutarch does draw together is more than sufficient for a comprehensive and psychologically intelligible portrait. Very early in his upbringing, writes Plutarch, Alexander displayed a temperament that was serious-minded and unattracted to excessive sensual pleasures. His all-consuming ambition was a simple one: to achieve great things in life. To suggest effectively Alexander's dedication to that goal, Plutarch recounts the lad's annoyance with each accomplishment attained by Philip. Plutarch phrases the matter this way: "For since he did not covet pleasure, nor even wealth, but excellence and fame, he considered that the more he should receive from his father the fewer would be the successes won by himself" (V, 235).

While still rather young, Alexander also gave evidence of a rigid mind of his own, a fact that led to fiery confrontations with his father, who was possessed of a similar constitution. Philip, at the same time, was perceptive enough to observe that his son's adamant positions were not mere signs of a strong will alone, for Alexander responded well when reasoned with. Rather than commanding the boy to obey, Philip brought in the most famed intellectual then living in the Hellenic world, Aristotle. No one except the best would qualify as tutor, guide, and confidant to Alexander, and Aristotle served in all these capacities to the young prince for many years. As a result, Alexander was well schooled and was brought to an enjoyment of reading and learning. Plutarch documents Alexander's knowledge, explaining that the young man became widely read in the works of Philistus, Euripides, Sophocles, Aeschylus, Telestus, and Philoxenus, in addition to Aristotle's own writing, of course.

Life with Philip remained a stormy business for Alexander in light of the unrelenting nature of each man. The two had numerous arguments, sometimes over the suitability of Alexander's friends (about whom Philip was very particular) and sometimes over Philip's extramarital love life. Eventually Philip's open amorous affairs proved fatal when the aggrieved Pausanias slew him. Plutarch implies that Olympias or Alexander may have encouraged Pausanias to the deed. Whatever the truth of the matter, Alexander, upon his father's death, reached a crucial watermark in his career, and this at an early age. Plutarch memorably analyzes the moment with these words:

Thus it was that at the age of twenty years Alexander received the kingdom, which was exposed to great jealousies, dire hatreds, and dangers on every hand. For the neighbouring tribes of Barbarians would not tolerate their servitude, and longed for their hereditary kingdoms; and as for Greece, although Philip had conquered her in the field, he had not had time enough to make her tame under his yoke. . . .[1] (XI, 251–53)

Never a man to flinch at troubles, Alexander acted swiftly and decisively. First, he put a speedy halt to the barbarian disturbances, overrunning their territories all the way to the Danube where he fought and beat Syrmus, king of the Triballi. Learning then of the Theban uprising and the continued provocation of Demosthenes on behalf of the Hellenic league, Alexander took his men through the Thermopylae pass to reach Thebes. Once there, Alexander offered a last chance of amnesty to the rebels. Audaciously though bravely, suggests Plutarch, the Thebans instead demanded that Alexander surrender to them. The result, which Plutarch states in greatly understated terms, was that Alexander set his men to work on the city. Before very long, Thebes was entirely annihilated. When, however, the razing of Thebes did not have the desired effect on her peoples and they still refused to acquiesce to the Macedonians, Alexander rounded up all the citizens except the priests, the descendants of Pindar (whom he revered), and those who had voted against the revolt. Those not exempted, however, thirty thousand in all, Alexander sold into slavery. Plutarch interrupts his revelations here to explain that later Alexander regretted having treated the Thebans so harshly; in fact he became reconciled with the Athenians not long afterward. Plutarch likened Alexander to the enraged lion that displays unlimited savagery for a time, only to become docile again once the anger has been expelled. In the case of Alexander, following his explosions of brutality, he often remitted all charges against his opponents and sought to make conciliatory amends.

Many of Alexander's military experiences centered around his engagements with Dareius, king of the Persians. Just as Mithridates had played the role of nemesis to several Roman commanders, Dareius proved frustrating to Alexander, who for years never could catch and conquer his adversary. Most of Alexander's early battles consequently stemmed from his pursuit of the elusive barbarian monarch. Plutarch excels at re-creating the martial ethos of such encounters, such as Alexander's initial confrontation with Dareius, which took place on the banks of the Granicus River. There, at the very threshold of Asia, the Persian generals had marshaled massive forces to catapult the Macedonians at once into a pitched fight. Plutarch underscores the fact that the psychological signficance of this opening encounter was absolutely clear to Alexander. Despite the advice of his military aides and though he thereby would seriously endanger his men, Alexander insisted that his army cross the river, since it symbolized so much to both sides. While Alexander drew attention to himself through conspicuous heroics, his men were enabled to bridge the river boundary safely and to thrust on into Persian territory. At this, the barbarian will to fight wilted, and Alexander had won the first round in a series of battles with the Persians.

The Macedonians seemed to hold the upper hand in their encounters with the adversary over a span of several years. But Alexander never was able to clinch the needed final triumph over Dareius. Climaxing their rivalry was a battle at Gaugamela where Dareius, with a reported one million men, awaited attack by Alexander. As Plutarch narrates the thrilling events, although his men were frightened of Dareius' superior numbers and sought only the most ideal circumstances before charging, Alexander refused the advice of his aides to engage the giant army only in the night. Instead, he pronounced what became his slogan, which, as repeated by Plutarch, went: "I will not steal my victory." Despite his favorable odds, Dareius then suffered a devastating defeat in the ensuing battle. The balance was tipped once and for all in favor of Alexander that day, records Plutarch. Soon thereafter Dareius was caught and slain, thus concluding the early phase of Alexander's warfare. As Plutarch relates the details, the reader can feel along with Alexander the hopes and anxieties that go into war.

No one ever has questioned Alexander's amazing military skill and personal courage, declares Plutarch. Many illustrations of Alexander's bravery are provided by the biographer, as when, for instance, he lagged behind his men to save his aged tutor Lysimachus who could not keep up. The two stragglers thereby became separated from the others, and Alexander was forced to hack their way through enemy lines to reach safety. Plutarch attributes much of his hero's success to his extraordinary control over the appetites of the senses. He quotes the Macedonian leader as having said that his tutor Leonidas "'used to come and open my chests of bedding and clothing to see that my mother did not hide there for me some luxury or superfluity'" (XXII, 289). To avoid extravagant foods, Alexander prescribed a limit of 10,000 drachmas for any meal of which he partook. Moreover, totally unlike many outstanding military figures who became involved in numerous amatory episodes, Alexander exercised self-mastery in that area as well. When he had captured Dareius' wife and daughters, his behavior toward them was impeccable; he had them lodged in safe, comfortable quarters where they were shown all the amenities. Plutarch viewed these courtesies as crucial indicators of Alexander's personal morality, wherein he considered the mastery of himself a more noble accomplishment than the mere conquest of his opponents. In the same connection, Plutarch repeats certain beliefs of Alexander concerning sleep and sexual intercourse which, the hero claimed, "more than any thing else, made him conscious that he was mortal, implying that both weariness and pleasure arise from one and the same natural weakness" (XXII, 287).

At the same time, Plutarch was not insensitive to fundamental flaws in the character of his favorite hero. Although he takes care to debunk lingering rumors of Alexander's excessive drinking, throughout most of the biography Plutarch still honestly relates the ugly implications when, after a long and leisurely dinner, Alexander would sit over wine for hours of conversation. During these sessions, he eventually would boast and bluster shamefully, all the while lending encouragement to the swarm of flatterers who would surround him at such times. Plutarch admitted, too, that Alexander's famed munificence, though usually the result of heart-felt affection or benevolence, on other occasions became simply an implement of his vanity. At those times, he would become furious with any men who sought to refuse his gifts, while calmly rewarding those more mercenary by nature who asked for things outright.

Without saying so explicitly, Plutarch nonetheless makes it known that beneath Alexander's misdemeanors lay excessive pride, an affliction not uncommon among those who wield immense power. For example, persons who would not agree with him benignly, Alexander viewed as troublemakers. Even former close friends to Alexander like Callisthenes, observes Plutarch, gradually were to become alienated from the monarch by not being obsequious at all times. The peril of candor before Alexander was evident, too, when Callisthenes was imprisoned and later rumored to have been killed by the ruler. A similar hostility toward Aristotle evolved in Alexander's relationship with him, continues Plutarch. In short, Alexander became increasingly merciless, a fact Plutarch documents extensively when recounting Alexander's later career in the Indian marches. When crack mercenary fighters among the Indians exacted a high toll on his forces, for instance, Alexander made a spurious peace pact with them. But the moment they lowered their defenses, he promptly violated the agreement by seizing and slaying them. At this point in his narrative, Plutarch refuses to attempt a rationalization for Alexander's ignoble, disgraceful conduct. Speaking for all civilized men, Plutarch judges the acts fairly, saying that such deeds stained Alexander's military career for good, though in most all other instances he waged war properly and like a king.

Nor was Alexander immune to stubbornness. Throughout most of his Indian campaign, Alexander had enjoyed relatively easy success in attaining his military objectives. When he and his men tried to cross the Ganges River, however, they encountered sharp resistance, whereupon his own soldiers lost their desire to go on further with the expedition. The prior steady diet of victories had not prepared Alexander for the resulting rebuff, and at first he made every effort to fire the enthusiasm of his men to continue the trek. But when he could not succeed, Alexander finally stopped sulking and turned his armies back toward their homeland. Rather than conveniently to ship the men and goods back by boat, however, Alexander overconfidently commanded that they march overland, contrary to the sound advice offered him. Alexander's miscalculations were to prove extremely costly, announces Plutarch. Frequent attacks by natives, short supplies of rations, and many strange diseases resulted in the decimation of Alexander's ranks, with three-quarters of the men lost.

Upon his return home from the prestigious but perilous Indian expeditions, Alexander was faced with a variety of vexing problems, most of which had accumulated during his lengthy sojourn in India. But he still was up to the task, and he quickly regained control over mutinous nations and over his dissatisfied kinsmen. Alexander settled the domestic complaints which were lowering morale in Persia and Macedonia and thereby re-established an equilibrium for the time being. But though the political alliances and arrangements had been mended, Alexander was disturbed by personal troubles. In particular, emphasizes Plutarch, he had become obsessed with superstition, which sapped his energy and distracted his thoughts. Certain omens disturbed him inordinately until, obsessed with the fear of dying, Alexander fell into a constant foul and morose moodiness. His pessimism was further intensified when a close companion, Hephaestion, suddenly died. Alexander for many days suffered extreme grief, as a consequence. Eventually, Alexander ceased mourning for his friend and instead commenced an extended session of solemn, excessive reveling with food and drink. Following one solid day of these bacchic carousings, Alexander became fatally feverish and soon thereafter died on June 13, 323 B.C.

In such a senseless fashion, lamented our biographer, the world-shaking reign of Alexander ended. Civilization, always in search of a genuine hero, thus lost one of its finest through an irresponsible spree. The tone of Plutarch's conclusion makes evident his personal moral disgust; once again a great man is brought low because of a lack of moderation and self-discipline. Nowhere in all his accounts does Plutarch hint that there exists any more effective alternatives to the humanists' doctrine of self-knowledge and use of reason to quell the passions. The case of Alexander's life would seem to prove his point.

CAESAR. Plutarch furnishes his readers with illuminating guideposts concerning Caesar's early life, just as he had with Alexander's. When Caesar was only a young man, Sulla, then dictator, commanded that he be killed. While fleeing to Bithynia for his life, the youth was captured by pirates whom he held in utter disdain. During captivity aboard their ship, Caesar casually wrote poetry, jested openly, and joined in their sports, as if to indicate to the cutthroats his complete lack of awe in the menacing circumstances. But once his ransom was paid and he was released, Caesar gathered a band of men and caught the sea thieves. Then, as the disbelieving brigands looked on in horror, their former captive had them crucified, a few at a time. By commencing his account of Caesar's life with this grim episode, Plutarch establishes from the start that his hero was a mighty figure to be reckoned with. Furthermore, Plutarch in this way defined the martial creed which marked the essence of Caesar's life: one who would live by the sword should be prepared also to die by the sword. In light of Caesar's infamous assassination years afterward, the connection of this early tale with Caesar's eventual death carried all the more impressive validity for Plutarch's readers.

Still, Caesar was no ordinary warrior. Plutarch also emphasizes Caesar's basic intelligence as well as his physical accomplishments. As was true with Plutarch's other favorite heroes, Caesar is portrayed as the complete man. Before he returned to Rome upon Sulla's death to pursue a military and political role, Caesar adhered to the essential humanistic doctrine of self-knowledge and self-cultivation. Specifically, he spent time in Rhodes studying philosophy and oratory with Apollonius, Cicero's former mentor. Plutarch further indicated that Caesar so perfected his public speaking that his future success in politics was assured. Nor did Caesar overlook the political advantages of smooth social intercourse with fellow Roman dignitaries once he began promoting his career. Caesar was psychologically aware of people and their needs and desires, as Plutarch stressed at the outset of his biography. Consequently, Plutarch's account of Caesar's rising career makes intriguing reading, because he anatomizes the deliberate tactics the young man practiced to gain popular support from his countrymen. Caesar nurtured his early career on a broad front. First, he earned an enthusiastic following by his eloquence as an advocate, hence reaping profit from his study with Apollonius. He also won good will from the commoners through the friendliness of his manner which, Plutarch testifies, Caesar carefully cultivated. At the same time, he rapidly increased political influence through lavish hospitality and ostentatious display in his manner of life. All these were factors which kept him perpetually in the forefront of society. In short, Caesar was conscious of his public image and undertook to make a public personality of himself, a process developed by politicians of all eras.

The first important stage in Caesar's lawmaking profession culminated about 63 B.C., in his successful candidacy for the post of high priest, or Pontifex Maximus, in an exceedingly close contest. Even during the beginning phases of his civilian influence, Caesar gave evidence of political adroitness; he lobbied openly for the consulship and unscrupulously contrived false alliances for the sake of expedient advantage. Because his tactics were too bold and direct, however, Caesar frequently was rebuffed in his early attempts for power. His ulterior intentions, overly obvious, alarmed his more republican-minded colleagues in legislative circles. The aristocracy in particular perceived that his maneuverings were aimed at their ruin. As Plutarch explained the issue, eventually the patricians refused even to attend Caesar's senate altogether, because he operated it so openly against their interests. Thus as Caesar's position in public evolved upward, his autocratic ambitions concerning the Empire elicited more and more mistrust among his fellow legislators. It was that matter which Plutarch explored thoroughly in his *Life of Caesar* and which Shakespeare was to project in his drama as the crux of Caesar's dilemma.

Caesar's lasting greatness, consequently, was to derive from his unparalleled feats on the battlefield, and not from his clumsiness in the stoa. Once he had climbed within reach of his paramount goal, dictatorship of Rome, Caesar, true to his name which in another form is known as "kaiser," relied more exclusively upon martial stratagems and less on hortative rhetoric. Further encouraging him to turn to military tactics, as Plutarch described the matter, was Caesar's unique dynamic leadership, which won him undying loyalty from soldiers, whereas his senatorial speeches succeeded only in antagonizing the established aristocracy of Rome. Plutarch devotes a large share of his commentary on Caesar to his hero's military fortes. Even in the earliest campaigns across the Alps and into Spain, Caesar displayed astute craft in warfare, a talent that enriched him and his men, since booty was the chief material reward for the enlisted fighter. Plutarch praised Caesar as second to none as a leader in war after recounting the Roman's performance in the campaigns in Gaul. In less than ten years of fighting there, he took over eight hundred cities, subdued three hundred nations, and fought battles against three million men (Plutarch's figures), killing one million of the enemy and capturing as many. Plutarch traces back such a spectacular record to concrete features of character:

Such spirit and ambition Caesar himself created and cultivated in his men, in the first place, because he showed, by his unsparing bestowal of rewards and honours, that he was not amassing wealth from his wars for his own luxury or for any life of ease, but that he treasured it up carefully as a common prize for deeds of valour, and had no greater share in the wealth than he offered to the deserving among his soldiers; and in the second place, by willingly undergoing every danger and refusing no toil. (XVII, 483)

As reported by Plutarch, Caesar's battles in Gaul and Europe stir the blood. He tells of Caesar's stratagems against the Helvetii and Nervii, and about his defeating their renowned leaders Abriorix and Vergentorix in pitched battles. The unmatched achievements of Caesar and his armies indicate an extraordinary skill and valor. In ten days, exclaims Plutarch, Caesar built a bridge across the rough Rhine River to become the first general to span that river with an army. On another front, he utilized his proven sea abilities to become "the first to launch a fleet upon the western ocean and to sail through the Atlantic sea carrying an army to wage war" (XXIII, 499). And in his efforts to subdue and occupy the islands comprising present-day Great Britain, Caesar carried the Roman banner beyond the very boundaries of the civilized world, declares Plutarch.

Caesar's fertile imagination also produced the most brilliant combined military and political coup recorded in all of history. Because of the significance of the deed, Plutarch dwells on the details at length. After the original uneasy alliance of Pompey, Caesar, and Crassus was dissolved with the latter's death among the Parthians, the remaining two strong men alone were left to compete for Rome. Pompey boldly announced his intention to be its dictator; and though Caesar's goal obviously was the same, he refused to declare his hopes in any brash manner as was once his wont. Instead, by suggesting a reasonable sounding ploy—namely, that both aspiring rulers leave their forces behind and rather to contend peaceably for the support of Rome and hence spare the city—Caesar won valuable time with Pompey. As Caesar rightfully reasoned, Pompey after all could have seized control because of larger forces than Caesar's; but with additional time, Caesar himself could better arm his men for the unavoidable confrontation ahead. Even so, however, a direct encounter with Pompey involved high risk, thought Caesar. During the pause from armed contention, therefore, Caesar concluded that his best hope was to frighten his enemies with a bold, unexpected enterprise, rather than attempt to overwhelm Pompey's forces. Plutarch outlined the plan, step by step. After appearing leisurely at a banquet in Rome before a large public audience, Caesar the same night streaked to the border between Cisalpine Gaul and the rest of Italy, a boundary designated by the river Rubicon. For a suspenseful moment in history Caesar deliberated about his own possible fate and that of Rome. Then, pronouncing the famed expression, "Let the die be cast," he raced across the river to take the startled city of Ariminum.

He had anticipated the results of the daring venture perfectly. All Italy along with Rome became senseless with panic; and Pompey, believing that all-out war had started, was fooled completely. Pompey declared a state of anarchy, dismissed all political deliberations, and fled, thereby vacating the seat of power in Rome. At first Caesar gave pursuit to Pompey's fleeing forces. But when his quarry sailed away from Brundisium, Caesar turned back to Rome, since he had no fleet. Plutarch marked the auspicious occasion in these words: ". . . so he turned back to Rome, having in sixty days and without bloodshed become master of all Italy" (XXXV, 529). The perceptive Plutarch also provided a rare touch of humor regarding those chaotic events. In particular, his narrative captured for all time the picture of Roman nobles streaming from the city in confusion: "Accordingly, the consuls fled, without even making the sacrifices usual before departure; most of the senators also fled, after seizing, in a sort of robbery, whatever came to hand of their own possessions, as though it were the property of others" (XXXIV, 527).

Upon assuming absolute command of Rome, Caesar moved at once to solidify his position, first by having the senate declare him dictator and then by bringing home exiles and relieving the debtor classes. Only then did he resume his pursuit of Pompey. After several inconclusive skirmishes, Caesar successfully beat Pompey's army. Mortified at the turn of events, Pompey slipped away into Egypt where ultimately he was murdered by an agent of Ptolemy. Then after an extended sojourn in Egypt, during which time he became involved in a notorious love affair with Cleopatra and led his final militiary campaign against Pompey's sons, Caesar returned to Rome. There, he treated himself to a gigantic triumphal procession and had himself ceremoniously appointed dictator of Rome for life. At this moment in Caesar's life, concludes Plutarch, he had become the most celebrated Roman of all time; he had proven his superiority both in senatorial machinations and on the battlefield. Caesar's name would be inscribed in every history book from that point on.

Without exception, in the heroes whose lives Plutarch traces there exist faults in character and judgment which run side by side with attributes of greatness. In the case of Caesar, Plutarch informs us, the most vocal opposition to him as a person derived from his obvious passion for royal power. It will be recalled, too, that Shakespeare constructed his epic tragedy of Caesar precisely upon this flaw. Many Roman citizens believed that Caesar slighted the responsibilities of the senate and the persons of the tribunes as well, a misgiving of too-great individual power shared by other Romans in other ages. Consequently, the people began to look longingly at Marcus Brutus for recourse, details about which Plutarch speaks fully in his biography of Brutus. A conspiracy gathered momentum; and as most readers are aware, Plutarch's accounts of this development were borrowed directly by Shakespeare sixteen hundred years later when he created his dramatic protagonists for *Julius Caesar*. For example, when Antony and Dolabella are accused to Caesar of plotting revolution, Plutarch quotes Caesar as having stated: "'I am not much in fear of these fat, long-haired fellows, but rather of those pale, thin ones,' meaning Brutus and Cassius" (LXII, 589). The parallel lines from Shakespeare's play are known to all readers. In addition, the incidents involving ill omens on the day of the killing, such as the Ides of March, the sacrifice without a heart, and Calpurnia's foreboding dream, all are found initially in Plutarch's narrative. It is instructive to notice, too, that Plutarch furnished Shakespeare even with the fatal psychological clues which explain why Caesar would have ventured forth to the senate in the first place on such an unpropitious day. Plutarch states that Caesar finally was convinced by Decimus Brutus to attend the fateful assembly because assumedly that day the senate was prepared to declare him king of all provinces outside Italy, along with the kingship of Italy itself which he already held. Shakespeare also was to indicate the over-reaching implications in Caesar's motives for attending the senate.

Plutarch's description of the actual assassination is consonant with various other accounts found in other of his *Parallel Lives*. Upon Caesar's arrival at the senate, many of the senators crowded around him on business, as was the usual custom. Cimber's pulling down of Caesar's cloak served as the signal for the conspirators, and Casca was first to strike. But Casca's first blow with a knife only resulted in a superficial stab on Caesar's neck, prompting the victim to grab the weapon and cry, "Accursed Casca, what doest thou?" (LXVI, 597). At this, the other murderers swarmed upon Caesar, flailing at him with their daggers. Although Shakespeare's words for Caesar ("Et tu, Brutus?") are not found here verbatim, an identical creation of the effects of the moment is derived from Plutarch's remark: "And it is said by some writers that although Caesar defended himself against the rest and darted this way and that and cried aloud, when he saw that Brutus had drawn his dagger, he pulled his toga down over his head and sank" (LXVI, 599).

The rest of Caesar's story was well known even as Plutarch wrote down the details—how the senators fled in panic but how Brutus' words of calm momentarily restored balance in Rome until Caesar's will was read, disclosing that he had given every Roman citizen a considerable gift. Following that disclosure, the conspirators played out their own horrific tales. In closing the *Life of Caesar*, Plutarch cast his thoughts back over the passion-filled episodes. He perceived the paradox whereby the most extraordinary mortal of the age could be removed so suddenly from the scene. The words of Plutarch still serve well today as Caesar's final epitaph:

> At the time of his death Caesar was fully fifty-six years old, while of the power and dominion which he had sought all his life at so great risks, and barely achieved at last, of this he had reaped no fruit but the name of it only, and a glory which had awakened envy on the part of his fellow citizens. (LXIX, 605)

The two contradictory themes inherent in Caesar's career in Plutarch's version, *memento mori* and compensatory glory for failed ambitions, have assured this biography fascinated readers in every civilized era since Plutarch put the words down on paper.

II *A Final Verdict on the* Lives

Naturally, a cursory review of a handful of the *Parallel Lives* does not entitle us to draw sweeping, absolute conclusions. At the same time, we may bring together certain key impressions derived from even the few specimen lives examined. The most impressive achievement evident in the *Lives* is Plutarch's sympathetic imagination. Unlike professional historians who might simply accumulate dates and deeds from which to draw an historical portrait of the times, Plutarch provides another dimension as well. With astonishing success, he enters into the very being of his characters in one of the world's outstanding feats of human empathy. As a result, the *Lives* read engagingly and smoothly, much as exciting stories.

In part, the engrossing quality of Plutarch's accounts can be attributed to the subjective perspective which the biographer employs—the same subjectivity, it should be observed, that disconcerts the historian coming to Plutarch's work. As we have noted already, Plutarch's reliance on a subjective viewpoint does not indicate that he consciously eschewed a detached position at all times. Rather, he blew a life breath into the brittle assemblage of details making up the contours of a life; this he achieved by attempting to comprehend entirely the hero concerned. The fact that Plutarch may or may not have personally liked the character is of no consequence. His narratives of the lives of Lysander and Sulla reflect the identical empathic exploration of soul as found in the stories of Alexander and Caesar, even though the former two personages were pronounced rascals by Plutarch. In every case the biographer works his way into the existence of his subject and expresses what he discerns from his special inner vantage point. In a subtle fashion, therefore, Plutarch psychoanalyzes his protagonist and thereby brings to the surface the key that is exactly fitted for opening the door to the man's character. Whereas historians might balk at the psychological hypotheses Plutarch formulates, the biographer is driven by a motive that is different. He wishes to reveal the "life" of the figure, not just the events associated with the life. Obviously, there is a risk involved in such an approach. But when Plutarch accurately gauges his subject, as he usually does in the *Parallel Lives*, his insights are invaluable. As one prime illustration, consider Plutarch's method of conveying the urgent sense of incompleteness which prompted Julius Caesar's ambitious drive:

> Caesar's successes . . . did not divert his natural spirit of enterprise and ambition to the enjoyment of what he had laboriously achieved, but served as fuel and incentive for future achievements, and begat in him plans for greater deeds and a passion for fresh glory, as though he had used up what he already had. What he felt was therefore nothing else than emulation of himself, as if he had been another man, and a sort of rivalry between what he had done and what he purposed to do. (LXVIII, 577)

Nor does Plutarch leave this last point a mere vague generality. He adds that among the projects in Caesar's mind were further invasions, profitable canals, land and swamp reclamation, harbors, and roads. In addition, he had the calendar studied and adjusted scientifically. Hence, one is tempted to declare that Plutarch incorporated the best of two worlds: that of the historian who revels in concrete data, and that of the biographer who quests for the soul of his subject.

Moreover, because the biographer aspires to delineate a life first and foremost, he will call upon whatever sources at his disposal that can assist him. In the case of Plutarch, this means we are treated to innumerable side glances at historical events connected with the hero of the biography. The separate life sketches, in fact, are better held together because of the incidentals. Rather than distracting the reader, they fill in, helping to complete the cosmos of the past. Thanks to the pieces of elaborative information Plutarch draws in while narrating the core life itself, the reader can sense the pulse of the times involved.

Almost never does Plutarch introduce such secondary details arbitrarily. The material possesses relevance to the life being discussed. Rather early in his consideration of Alexander, Plutarch clarifies the complex quality of Alexander's personality in terms of the "humour" theory often cited in recorded history. For example, the theory earlier in time had been promulgated by Theophrastus; later it appeared in medieval medicine; and still later the concept showed up in the drama esthetics of Ben Jonson and others. Plutarch similarly points to the humours belief to account for Alexander's moodiness:

Now, the cause of this, perhaps, was the temperament of his body, which was a very warm and fiery one; for fragrance is generated, as Theophrastus thinks, where moist humours are acted upon by heat. Wherefore the dry and parched regions of the world produce the most and best spices; for the sun draws away the moisture which, like material for corruption, abounds in vegetable bodies. And in Alexander's case, it was the heat of his body, as it would seem, which made him prone to drink, and choleric. (IV, 233)

Topics of incidental appropriateness furthermore add to the intrigue and interest of the *Lives*. In another vein, for instance, a long-standing tradition even in Plutarch's day was the lifting of brides across the threshold. The origin of that convention (which still remains with us) is casually related by Plutarch while he ostensibly comments on Romulus' motives in the rape of the Sabine women: "And it continues to be a custom down to the present time that the bride shall not of herself cross the threshold into her new home, but be lifted up and carried in, because the Sabine women were carried in by force, and did not go in of their own accord" (XV, 133–35). Even the theory of immaculate conception is dealt with in Plutarch's story of Numa, but again solely as a secondary issue. When Numa's wife Tatia died, recounts Plutarch, the widower left the city to reside in the quiet countryside, giving rise to rumors that he had found perfect bliss there by living with a goddess, Egeria. Though he personally expresses skepticism about the arrangement, Plutarch acknowledges that the Egyptians apparently once believed in such a union of divinity and mortal, at least to a degree. Plutarch in passing declares, "And yet the Aegptians make a distinction here which is thought plausible, namely, that while a woman can be approached by a divine spirit and made pregnant, there is no such thing as carnal intercourse and communion between a man and a divinity" (IV, 317–19).

Finally, that Plutarch would not use subterfuge to conceal his strong ethical foundations is to be appreciated. As he relates the events and explains the personalities of his subjects, we are perfectly aware that, tacitly, Plutarch judges them on the basis of a *right* and *wrong* which he believed existed in our universe. Archbishop Trench arrived at the same conclusion in his purview of Plutarch, when he wrote: "Vivid moral portraiture, this is what he aimed at, and this is what he achieved. It is not too much to affirm that his leading purpose in writing these LIVES was not historical, but ethical. More or less of historical background he was obliged to give to the portraits which he drew; but always and altogether in subordination to the portrait itself." [2]

If Plutarch is viewed as free from the inappropriate strictures of the historian and instead is seen as biographer of the total man, both body and soul, reservations concerning him vanish. We then can judge him as storyteller of men's lives, which was the very role he claimed he was playing. Today, the unique worth of such an aim still is claimed by one of America's finest biographers, Leon Edel, who recently wrote: "Your novelist and your biographer stand on this common ground—both are, in reality, storytellers. They simply tell different kinds of stories." [3]

CHAPTER 4

The Moralia *of Plutarch*

TURNING to the almost eighty different essays comprising the *Moralia,* the reader recognizes that the title does not account for the variety of commentaries involved. The name *Moralia,* or *Morals,* as they sometimes are designated, initially was applied to about twenty articles which dealt specifically with topics of an ethical nature. When additional pieces without a strictly moral bent were added to the collection later, the title never was altered to accommodate the augmented contents. No reader therefore should expect mere ethical elucidation from Plutarch's *Moralia;* rather, as with his *Lives,* these essays touch upon innumerable daily concerns and personages. Called "the first essayist," Plutarch here reflects successfully the aura of the Roman-Hellenic world of his day.[1] And because of their "combination of charm, scholarship, and worldly wisdom," the *Moralia* have attracted readers down the ages, and with them translators such as Sir Thomas Elyot and Erasmus.[2]

Readers today are at a handicap regarding the *Moralia* because, as classicists tell us, we possess only about half the studies Plutarch wrote, just as we have possibly half the number of *Lives* he set down. Still, the picture of his times which Plutarch creates when the *Lives* and the *Moralia* are taken together grants us a more humane perspective of that age which frequently has become better known in the cynical accounts of Juvenal, Tacitus, and Suetonius, who concentrated on the darker side of human nature. Our comprehension and appreciation of Plutarch's portraitures would be much improved if we acknowledge that the *Lives* and *Moralia* together constitute Plutarch's vision. Archbishop Trench realized the complementary nature of Plutarch's two large bodies of writing one hundred years ago, in remarking that "the one half setting forth to us, and, so far as this is possible, from ideal points of view, what the ancient world had accomplished in the world of action, and the other what, in like manner, it had accomplished in the world of thought." [3]

As was true with the *Lives*, we cannot be positive regarding dates and the circumstances of the writing of the *Moralia*. Among classical scholars the general consensus is that they were composed before the *Lives*, some probably while Plutarch resided in Rome lecturing and fulfilling his diplomatic duties, towards the end of the first century A.D. Those pieces most distinctly moralistic, for example, probably had been lecture notes. Such topics as are covered there—*The Education of Children, How to Tell a Flatterer from a Friend, How to Profit by One's Enemies,* and the like—would fit within the limits of philosophy, Plutarch's avowed area of study. We also know that Plutarch, as a matter of course, continued all his life to take notes on his observations from books or life itself. The result was countless well-stocked notebooks from which to draw. Though he possessed an excellent memory, Plutarch at the same time shows few signs of relying solely upon his recollections. Instead, whenever he found the opportunity, he read and consulted books, taking down specific details or quotations which later were to appear in his works.[4]

It remains axiomatic that a reader cannot hope to fathom the essence of Plutarch's accomplishment in the *Moralia* without reading them in their entirety, particularly because of the random nature of the separate topics. For our purposes here, we shall distinguish a few significant categories into which the majority of the *Moralia* fit logically without pretending to catalogue each essay rigidly or absolutely. A scrutiny of the individual articles shows that Plutarch's interests lay principally in personal behavior, in discussions of various cultural phenomena of the Greeks, Romans, and Egyptians, in cosmological speculations, and in religio-metaphysical commentaries. In addition, there were countless studies of a more miscellaneous character, such as Plutarch's criticisms of poetry and particular authors, his appreciation of the courage displayed by some women in history, and his thoughts on different political systems. To approach the *Moralia* in the most effective way possible, therefore, we shall consider selected essays under headings paralleling Plutarch's interests: "Morals," "Customs," "Cosmology," "Metaphysics," and "Random Concerns."

I *Morals*

On the basis of what we already have learned about Plutarch, it is wholly consistent that the largest single magnetic pole in the *Moralia* be comprised of essays treating personal conduct. On many occasions in the *Lives,* Plutarch showed himself first and above all a moral philosopher. His own life, too, we earlier observed, reflected a primal belief that, by precept and by example, teaching men how to lead a better life was a worthy undertaking. He accomplished that instruction both through his writings and the scrupulous discipline of his life as civic and religious guide. Plutarch, we will recall, "himself regarded public life as providing the fullest opportunity for the exercise of moral qualities." [5] And in his capacities as emissary abroad, minor magistrate at Chaeronea, and official at Delphi, Plutarch left an imprint on a variety of persons, a fact revealed indirectly in the *Moralia.*

Almost a third of the *Moralia* readily qualify as ethical edification. In the Loeb editions of the *Moralia,* which will become the first English version of the entire *Moralia* when completed, nearly every piece found in LCL volumes I, II, VI, X, and VII relates to proper personal decorum. The forms taken by those writings are varied: advice directed to actual people on a multitude of subjects, usually in an epistolary form; letters to specific persons, addressed by name; fictitious dialogues among several friends; and simple expository essays as we still write today. The contents of the separate studies are even more varied than the formats. A layman's medical advice, for example, constitutes *Advice About Keeping Well.*[6] Though medicine interested Plutarch in a nonprofessional sense, this brief essay makes no attempt to usurp the physician's more formal directives. Plutarch simply speaks as a well-intentioned friend, taking into account matters of diet, sleep, bathing, exercise, and preventative health measures. The key to good health, advises Plutarch, is moderation in all things, even though that elusive balance may be difficult "in the midst of company and good cheer." He rationally supports his plea for moderation in food, drink and bodily pleasures by arguing that immoderations injure one's health and thus ultimately curb one's ability to partake in enjoyable activities: "Hence contempt for health is least profitable for those who make pleasure their chief aim" (II. 8. 237). Plutarch's theories about sleep and dreams reflect the thoughts of a cultivated man in the ancient past derived from a quasimedical system of humours. One should seek a night's sleep with few interruptions. If someone's dreams are abnormal or improper, there must be "an over-abundance or concentration of humours, or a disturbance of spirit within" (II. 14. 251–53), which echoes his comment in the *Life of Alexander* concerning the dangers of imbalanced humours. In his homey view of the body, Plutarch further intimates that uneasy sleep might anticipate an impending physiological ailment, because "the emotions of the soul have often given warning that the body is perilously near disease" (II. 14. 253).

Plutarch lays special emphasis on diet and exercise in *Advice About Keeping Well.* One peculiar position he holds is that meat is not a natural need of the body; in fact, meat is "dulling to the reasoning faculty, which, as it were, is kindled from plain and light substances" (II. 18. 265). On the other hand, he encourages the drinking of wine (in moderation, of course) as "the most beneficial of beverages, the pleasantest of medicines, and the least cloying of appetizing things" (II. 19. 265). The quiescent man of scholarship, he further advises, should lessen his appetite, since he will have less need of nutrition (II. 20). But whether placid or not in one's living habits, exercise is called for. Massaging is useful in that respect, as are singing, dancing, and simply speaking (II. 16). Clearly, Plutarch believes that the inert man lives but minimally, which in turn brings him back to a central thesis about aiding one's fellow men. Near the conclusion of the essay, he summarizes the issue of maintaining sound physical well-being: "For health is not to be purchased by idleness and inactivity, which are the greatest evils attendant on sickness, and the man who thinks to conserve his health by uselessness and ease does not differ from him who guards his eyes by not seeing, and his voice by not speaking. For a man in good health could not devote himself to any better object than to numerous humane activities" (II. 24. 281).

Sounding every bit like a sociology textbook on marriage is Plutarch's piece called *Advice to Bride and Groom.* Dedicated to Pollianus and Eurydice, a newly wedded couple obviously known well to Plutarch, the essay (which may have been a letter) makes the crucial point that physical attraction alone, or what we today call infatuation, is insufficient for a lasting married relationship.

Another ingredient—Reason again—is mandatory, writes Plutarch, who was himself a happy husband and father: ". . . the keen love between newly married people that blazes up fiercely as the result of physical attractiveness must not be regarded as enduring or constant, unless, by being centred about character, and by gaining a hold upon the rational faculties, it attains a state of vitality" (II. 4. 303). Although the husband should rule the household and the wife acquiesce in the husband's choice of friends and religion, the healthy marriage, states Plutarch, demands the acceptance of a partnership relationship. Anticipating civil law by centuries, Plutarch asserts that in the partnership of marriage, all goods and resources are to be seen as mutually possessed, just as are the resulting children (II. 20). Meanwhile, the discreet wife should remain quiet and keep at home, devoting all her being to serving the husband. Should the husband become irate about some matter, Plutarch urges a psychological approach as valid now as it was then: "Women who have sense keep quiet while their husbands in their fits of anger vociferate, but when their husbands are silent they talk to them and mollify them by words of comfort" (II. 37. 327).

Students of Renaissance letters will recognize the genre represented by Plutarch's *To an Uneducated Ruler* (Vol. X).[7] An essay giving advice to kings or heads, this piece resembles in many ways the standard didactic works for rulers written during the Renaissance, such as Machiavelli's *The Prince*, Castiglione's *The Courtier*, Elyot's *The Book of the Governor*, Lydgate's *Fall of Princes*, and Baldwin's *Mirror for Magistrates*. Whether or not the fragment we possess was originally part of one of Plutarch's lectures or a letter written to a particular monarch is not known. Whatever its inception, in the opening as we have it, Plutarch appears fully aware of the difficulties in winning the ear of kings because, as he writes, ". . . they are afraid to accept reason as a ruler over them, lest it curtail the advantage of their power by making them slaves to duty" (X. 1. 53). Thus Plutarch deftly prepares his argument by accusing stubborn leaders of eschewing the rational because it makes them subject to an authority beyond their personal whim. Plutarch then claims that the head who insists his people act properly must prove himself worthy of emulation. Throughout both the *Lives* and the *Moralia*, Plutarch helps make his points comprehensible through incisive figures of speech. The king in this specific metaphor becomes a straight-edge ruler whose own shape must be held firm if those to be guided are expected to be unswerving: "But just as a rule, if it is made rigid and inflexible, makes other things straight when they are fitted to it and laid alongside it, in like manner the sovereign must first gain command of himself, must regulate his own soul and establish his own character, then make his subjects fit his pattern" (X. 2. 55–57). Plutarch thereby introduces the prerequisite for ruling well: self-control, which permits Reason to operate. Reason, in turn, is made analogous to ballast in the metaphorical ship of state, keeping the ship paced and on an even keel, "thus by greater slowness ensuring the safety of its course" (X. 6. 69).

One is forced to dissent with a recent scholar who claims that this essay, though once an "educative force," has lost its effectiveness in the Western world since absolute monarchies have vanished.[8] Plutarch, after all, was expounding a system which involved a total worldly and metaphysical hierarchy; whether the man at the top is called a king or a president is secondary. Rather, the ruler governs according to a law which Plutarch touches upon: "Now justice is the aim and end of law, but law is the work of the ruler, and the ruler is the image of God who orders all things" (X. 3. 59). Beneath Plutarch's short and seemingly straightforward advice is the adumbration of a divine order derived from his principal master, Plato. In the last analysis, of course, nothing radically new is proposed here. But *To an Uneducated Ruler* shows clearly how earlier thought continued through the blood stream of the civilized world centuries after its initial conception.

Two essays almost certainly originally written as letters are *A Letter of Condolence to Apollonius* and *Consolation to His Wife*. Both pieces were designed to offer comfort to someone bereaved, and the letter form for conveying that sentiment was frequently employed by others besides Plutarch; Plato, Seneca, Cicero, Lucretius, and Crantor all had written well-known letters of solace, for example. The latter message, as indicated by the title, was addressed to his wife Timoxena when Plutarch learned that their only daughter, two-year-old Timoxena, had died while he was away from home at Tanagra. Though we possess other drafts of this letter, it appears that the manuscript usually translated (as in the Loeb editions) was Plutarch's final version and undoubtedly was not even intended to be included in his literary corpus. The message addressed to Apollonius is different. The lack of warmth in that epistle suggests that the connections between Plutarch and his correspondent may not have been especially strong or that the manuscript used for the modern translations was but a rough draft of some final letter. Nonetheless, both writings bear similar workbench marks.

At first it might seem that Plutarch speaks in both epistles from the Stoic point of view; he admonishes excessive outcry from either Apollonius or Timoxena. With Apollonius, Plutarch appeals to his sense of manly dignity, stating that "It is the mark of educated and disciplined men to keep the same habit of mind toward adversity" (II. 4. 113–15). His counsel to his wife is much more intimate, as expected, and she is warned that extreme sorrow on her part will only distress him all the more. He appeals to her to help him during the dark hours: "Only, my dear wife, in your emotion keep me as well as yourself within bounds. For I know and can set a measure to the magnitude of our loss, taken by itself; but if I find any extravagance of distress in you, this will be more grievous to me than what has happened" (VII. 2. 581).[9] Yet in neither instance does Plutarch go on to develop the traditional Stoic stance that good or ill fortune in life is meaningless. Plutarch's profound faith in the power of Reason comes into play, with Apollonius in more distant, universal terms, while with Timoxena in a more familial context of decorum (see VII. 4. 587). Apollonius is reminded that "Reason is the best remedy for the cure of grief, reason and the preparedness through reason for all the changes of life" (II. 6. 119). Such words lead to the pervasive humanistic doctrine by now familiar to readers of our essayist-biographer: "The measure of life is its excellence, not its length in years" (II. 17. 159).

In turning to *The Dinner of the Seven Wise Men,* we encounter a specimen of Plutarch's dialogue technique. Actual dinner parties, where good acquaintances gather for a repast followed by extended, leisurely conversation, of course were common long before Plutarch's age and remain popular still. In writing down some of the issues of commentary in the form of literary dialogues, Plutarch was blazing no new trails. Plato often took the format of such meetings for his writings, to name only the best-known earlier exponent of the pattern. *The Dinner of the Seven*

Wise Men does, however, represent an innovation on its author's part, for in writing about such a dinner attended by the traditional wise men, Plutarch was perpetuating a model put forth several centuries earlier by Plato and Xenophon, who had written their dialogues about the same legendary wise men. Beginning with a tradition reported by Plato in the *Protagoras* that the seven wise men met at Delphi for the dedication of the two most famous inscriptions on the temple, Plutarch fashioned his imaginary symposiac dealing with the same occasion and same participants.[10]

At the outset of the piece Plutarch spends several pages in establishing the setting for the events. A narrator, Diocles, is provided a listener, Nicarchus, thus allowing for the two-way discussion of details of the famed dinner. Not just the wise men at first, but instead many participants people Plutarch's landscape. They gather near the shrine of Aphrodite in Delphi where the fête is to be held. Carriages are said to have been sent for the guests, and at that time of the streets all about are crowded, much like many scenes in Petronius' *Satyricon.* Once the scene has been set and the important dignitaries introduced to the reader, Plutarch follows through the rest of the evening simply reporting, or recording, the discussions.

Before and during dinner, casual comments are made on such topics as the responsibility of the man invited to dinner for taking an active part in the conversations, the cause for a deformed newborn horse on the host's estate, and the plainness of fare brought for the wise men (II. Parts 2–4). A highlight of the evening commences when Neiloxenus is invited to read aloud the message he has brought from Amasis, king of Egypt, for Bias, one of the wise men. The message in fact turns out to be a kind of riddle which Bias, as a learned man, is asked to answer. The king of the Ethiopians, writes King Amasis, has challenged him to an impossible deed, "to drink up the ocean," which, if complied with, would earn Amasis many villages and towns of the Ethiopian. But if Amasis was stymied by the request, then he would "withdraw from the towns lying about Elphantine" (II. 6. 375). With little loss of time, Bias responds with an answer for Amasis that would quite confound the Ethiopian king in return: "'Well, then,' said Bias, 'let him tell the Ethiopian to stop the rivers which are now emptying into the ocean depths, while he himself is engaged in drinking up the ocean that now is; for this is the ocean with which the demand is concerned, and not the one which is to be' " (II. 6. 377).

That the Ethiopian ruler should so pass his time with cryptic requests instead of governing his people leads the wise men to thoughts about leadership. On that note, Thales, Bias, Pittacus, Anacharsis, Solon, Chilon, and Cleobulus all agree to offer opinions on how best to rule a government. The viewpoint of each is expressed succinctly: Solon, for instance, states, " 'In my opinion either a king, or a despot, would best gain repute if out of a monarchy he should organize a democracy for his people,' " while Pittacus says, " 'If the ruler should manage to make his subjects fear, not him, but for him' " (II.7. 379–81).

Amasis in turn had conveyed profound questions to the Ethiopian questioner which, when read before the gathered wise men, provided them with much to contemplate: What is the oldest thing? What is the greatest? What is the wisest? the most beautiful? the most common? and so on. Inasmuch as such queries plumb some significant facets of man's life, the philosophical discussions that ensued reflected much of the civilized man's mind of Plutarch's own age.

Gorgus' entrance to the company (II. 17. 427) prompts a series of unusual stories dealing with the benevolence of dolphins. Gorgus, who had been away on a mission to make a religious sacrifice, relates Arion's rescue from murderers on ship by dolphins who had heard his farewell song to life before throwing himself overboard to avoid the killers' knives. Swimming beneath his sinking body, the sea animals bore Arion upward until he was conveyed to the surface, as though riding the waves. Diocles suggests that the dolphin tales derived from an old-standing one; Ino earlier had thrown herself into the sea and had become metamorphosed into a sea goddess. Others present had similar stories to tell: Solon relates about Hesiod's unjust death being righted when dolphins retrieved his body from the ocean, and Pittacus recounts the saving of Enalus and his love by dolphins.

The final subject pondered late that evening, Diocles explains, was the significance of the three well-known inscriptions on Apollo's temple at Delphi: "Avoid extremes," "Know thyself," and "Give a pledge, and mischief attends" (II. 21. 447). Cursory answers are put forth by those still engrossed in the conversations, though no firm pronouncements are voiced. Then the dinner is over abruptly. Thus, the dinner format used was more than a simple device to bring together conversationalists. With the wisest men of ancient Greece assembled, matters of the greatest profundity could be considered eclectically. For Plutarch, the social implications of the group—intelligent friends brought together to exchange ideas in a spirit of fellowship—are as important as any strictly intellectually esoteric pronouncements. As Plutarch has Cleodorus say about the rites and institution of social dining, ". . . when the table is done away with, there go with it . . . the most humane and the first acts of communion between man and man" (II. 15. 417), a point of view Plutarch also repeats in opening his *Table-Talk*.

By far the largest proportion of essays which are predominantly didactic in spirit are written as lectures. Plutarch's manner with them is absolutely straightforward, with no literary superstructure superimposed or narrators involved. He speaks directly to his reader in a rational fashion, hoping by the weight of his logic and the potency of his illustrations to convince by the wisdom of his advice. *How to Tell a Flatterer from a Friend*, though not a long piece, contains cogent arguments concerning the perils of those seeking to ingratiate themselves. Plutarch shows the pragmatic side of his nature in warning readers against the conceit in each of them, for "it is because of this self-love that everybody is himself his own foremost and greatest flatterer" (I. 1. 265); thus each man is susceptible.[11] The flatterer, Plutarch continues, uses man's inclination to believe the best of himself in order to formulate close bonds with his victim. Such a process directly opposes the central doctrine of humanism, "Know Thyself," by developing "in every man deception towards himself and ignorance both of himself and of the good and evil that concerns himself" (I. 1. 267).

For Plutarch, a flatterer is a vicious enemy to be identified and then rooted out. He admits that locating the flatterer is not easy because he usually takes on the guise of a friend. But he must be discovered all the same, and Plutarch sets forth a campaign to trick the flatterer into revealing himself. Since the flatterer seeks to ingratiate himself by subtly imitating one in manner and in thought, Plutarch suggests that the suspect be watched carefully to learn whether he ever disagrees with one he emulates and whether he shifts his position on an issue to match his victim's. The true friend, on the other hand, "is neither an imitator of everything nor ready to commend everything, but only the best things . . ." (I. 9. 287). When the flatterer does disagree or speaks frankly, it is only in an instance that no hurt or pain is felt by his victim. Throughout the essay, in fact, Plutarch cautions against a too casual selection of one's friends in the first place. Exchanging secret confidences, for example, creates a form of bond between parties which makes retreating from the intimate relationship extremely difficult since the other knows one's personal affairs (I. 9. 291). Ultimately, the true identity of a friend or a flatterer will become exposed in his service, whether it be honorable or otherwise. But lest the final proof result in harm to the object of the flattery, Plutarch returns to his own credo for right living, a continual self-evaluation leading to self-knowledge. When we are fully cognizant of our own nature, we cannot be misled by honeyed statements and thus ". . . we shall not very readily let the flatterers walk over us" (I. 25. 349).

In *On Having Many Friends*, an essay almost certainly a lecture in its original shape, Plutarch resumes his explorations into man's social relationships, particularly those built upon a personal basis. Many of the same thoughts found in *The Dinner of the Seven Wise Men* and in *How to Tell a Flatterer from a Friend* appear here. As he remarked many times elsewhere, Plutarch says that a steadfast friend is very hard to come by, so that it is foolish to seek many friends and discard the old ones. Nor is the number of friends of utmost importance. As we come to expect of him, Plutarch reinforces a general statement with an analogue that precisely captures his idea: "But the flies do not stay on after the good food is gone, nor the retainers after their patron's usefulness is gone" (II. 3. 53)—a saying clearly dramatized in a play like *King Lear*. Nor should we make friends of chance acquaintances. Since a valid friendship is a valuable commodity, it should be established with care, and "we should seek after those who are worthy of friendship" (II. 4. 55).

Central to Plutarch's thesis concerning legitimate alliances between friends are both ethical and utilitarian factors, concepts alluded to obliquely in the piece on flatterers. In his *On Having*

Many Friends, however, Plutarch outlines the role of friendships in a man's life. By so doing, he makes clear why the trustworthy friend is a rarity and therefore needs to be sought out:

But true friendship seeks after three things above all else: virtue as a good thing, intimacy as a pleasant thing, and usefulness as a necessary thing, for a man ought to use judgement before accepting a friend, and to enjoy being with him and to use him when in need of him, and all these things stand in the way of one's having many friends. . . . (II. 3. 53)

How to Profit by One's Enemies, another of Plutarch's brief pieces, shows the other side of the coin. Here, the positive use of one's enemies is discussed in such an agreeable fashion that Christian moralists from the sixth century on have borrowed the essay for their own teachings. Again by means of a parallel—enemies like fire can be helpful once they are approached properly—Plutarch expounds on the process of turning one's ill-will to one's own good. First, he writes, foes keep one on his toes. They force one to appraise every deed and to do one's best. Surely it is not a bad thing "to have to live circumspectly, to give heed to one's self, and not to do or say anything carelessly or inconsiderately, but always to keep one's life unassailable as though under an exact regimen" (II. 3. 11). In addition, the attacks of an enemy against one's character may be turned to good advantage if the victim thereby is alerted to a legitimate fault not recognized before (II. 7. 25). And finally, half in earnest and half in jest, Plutarch points out that learning to tolerate unjust accusations from others is good training in mastering one's own passions. He puts it this way: "If you once acquire the habit of bearing an enemy's abuse in silence, you will very easily bear up under a wife's attack when she rails at you, and without discomposure will patiently hear the most bitter utterances of a friend or a brother . . ." (II. 8. 29).

On Listening to Lectures was first delivered as a lecture and only subsequently set down in writing for the young Nicander who was coming of age. The opening sentences of the essay state these facts along with Plutarch's humanistic position concerning the place of Reason in man's life. When the piece is distilled, we find the content closely related to the rest of Plutarch's didactic corpus, with reasonable guidelines concerning proper studying offered the young man going off to college.

The first point made is a simple one but crucial: serious learning is predicated on one's ability to listen and learn before attempting to speak anything of consequence. Listening, as the title implies, is a critical process which must be mastered. One cannot listen well, adds Plutarch, if he frequently interrupts with contradictions. Instead, Plutarch pleads for silent hearing of all that is said, after which a thoughtful person will be able to discern what is valuable and what is dross. In that way, one shows himself "to be a lover of truth and not a lover of disputation" (I. 4. 215). Plutarch also cautions against permitting one's envy to stand in the way of learning from a speaker, "because envious persons are pleased with anything rather than with the good points of a discourse" (I. 5. 215). Predisposed envious auditors who allow themselves to be distracted are captured in Plutarch's incisive description, as apt today as when he wrote it. Such an inferior listener, Plutarch writes, ". . . does not ponder upon any point of the discussion, but proceeds to count as votes the comments and attitudes of those present; if any approve, fleeing and recoiling from these as though frantic; if any disapprove or distort the things said, hastening to join their company . . ." (I. 5. 217).

Plutarch is equally acute in setting down the portrait of the poseur who remains unimpressed and unconvinced by anything stated. These auditors are too self-oriented to glean even a whit of information:

An offensive and tiresome listener is the man who is not to be touched or moved by anything that is said, full of festering presumption and ingrained self-assertion, as though convinced that he could say something better than what is being said, who neither moves his brow nor utters a single word to bear witness that he is glad to listen, but by means of silence and an affected gravity and pose, seeks to gain a reputation for poise and profundity; as though commendation were money, he feels that he is robbing himself of every bit that he bestows on another. (I. 13. 237)

At the same time, Plutarch does not encourage indiscriminate awarding of praise. Anyone having attended a public talk will recognize the person described by Plutarch as "light-minded and flighty, who uses no judgement, but hangs on every word and syllable," the too-eager applauder who only frustrates the speaker while annoying the audience, "startling them as he does and exciting them to join him contrary to their judgement, as though they for shame could not help being dragged into the applause" (I. 13. 239).

Plutarch reserves his most emphatic warnings regarding an honest evaluation of the lecture and the lecturer. Anticipating Marshall McLuhan by a good number of centuries, he employs another of his famed analogues to suggest that the showy manner easily can override the substance of a lecture or performance: "For as most of the mistakes of persons singing to the flute escape the audience, so an exuberant and impressive style flashed upon the listener blinds him to the matter set forth" (I. 7. 223).[12] What Plutarch argues is the standard position in esthetics from antiquity till the recent era of art for art's sake: no work of art or performance is of worth unless the content itself conveys a positive good, the long-standing *to teach and to delight* dictum. The point as phrased by Plutarch states: "Let the young man, then, find pleasure when he finds profit from a discourse; but he should not hold that the pleasure derived from the lecture is an end in itself" (I. 9. 227–29).

There is decorum involved in hearing lectures, and Plutarch makes clear his insistence that the speaker be shown due respect, whatever may be said for the talk. When sitting in the audience, for instance, the auditor has as much responsibility for correct eye contact as has the lecturer. The hearer must show "friendliness" in his bearing by way of a gentle glance, a serene countenance, or perhaps simply a face free from any trace of annoyance (I. 13. 243). But even if the lecture is a total failure, Plutarch contends that the "general and common requirements at every lecture" remain in effect; namely: "To sit upright without any lounging or sprawling, to look directly at the speaker, to maintain a pose of active attention, and a sedateness of countenance free from any expression, not merely of arrogance or displeasure, but even of other thoughts and pre-occupations" (I. 13. 243). Plutarch masterfully closes out his commentary by reminding young Nicander and all his readers that the human mind is not like a sponge to be filled—again his metaphoric illustration—but rather like wood requiring only "kindling to create in it an impulse to think independently and an ardent desire for the truth" (I. 18. 257–59).

Similar in many respects to the instructions given for listening to lectures is the essay called *The Education of Children,* a rather rambling piece covering much ground and frequently digressing from the announced subject. Plutarch here goes to the heart of the humanistic and moralistic spirit: to the teaching of children. Expounding a surprisingly refined form of educational and behavioral psychology for his day, he first establishes the ultimate aim for all education, what he calls "perfectly right action." From there he discusses what is needed to produce that goal: Nature, or first beginnings; Reason, by way of the act of learning; and Habit, by way of constant practice (I. 4. 9). The parallels between those prerequisite elements and, respectively, heredity, environment, and repeated conditioning are not difficult to discern. Because everything depends on this triumvirate, according to Plutarch, he amplifies how best to attain the best Nature, Reason and Habit. As for Nature, parentage is critical. Plutarch cautions the would-be father to avoid consorting with loose women since any children thus resulting could not possibly turn out well.[13] If the mother cannot herself nurse the child, which is the preferred arrangement for knitting bonds between parents and offspring, then a nursemaid must be chosen with great care lest the child be contaminated while still very impressionable. For best results, such a nurse should be at least Greek in character, if not nationality. Nor should the teacher be selected with any less caution. He should have impeccable manners, be free from any personal scandal, and possess wide teaching experience. And should the parent begrudge paying well for such a mentor for his child, then he will be assuring ignorance as the consequence, a commodity "which is cheap enough."

Plutarch's view of human existence resembles Plato's in several respects, not the least of which is his emphasis on the mind. Though he does not denigrate the body since, after all, it needs to be exercised for fitness, firmness, and discipline, Plutarch cautions that the training of the physical portion of man must not impinge upon the intellectual learning process: "But the amount of bodily exercise should be so limited as not to be a drain on the children and make them too tired to study; for, according to Plato, sleep and weariness are the enemies of learning" (I. 11. 39). For Plutarch, learning stands as the most marvelous and lasting process in the world because it deals with mind and reason, the two supreme elements in man's nature: "The mind exercises control over reason, and reason is the servant of the mind, unassailable by fortune, impregnable to calumny, uncorrupted by disease, unimpaired by old age" (I. 8. 25). Teaching, then, cultivates the mind which guides man's reason. All these contribute to man's leading the good life.

Again Plutarch does not stray far from the positions taken by his Greek philosopher forebears. The expansive, purposely flexible expression "leading the good life" was for earlier philosophers the prime subject of consideration, along with establishing guiding principles to its attainment. Not surprisingly, as a consequence, Plutarch considers philosophy the "head and front of all education" in his treatise on educating the young. The student of ethical systems from the Far East will see affinities between the tenets found, for example, in Confucian aphorisms and Plutarch's credo which states:

For through philosophy and in company with philosophy it is possible to attain knowledge of what is honourable and what is shameful, what is just and what is unjust, what, in brief, is to be chosen and what to be avoided, how a man must bear himself in his relations with the gods, with his parents, with his elders, with the laws, with strangers, with those in authority, with friends, with women, with children, with servants. . . . (I. 10. 35)

Plutarch's essay continues to detail other facets of the learning business, urging students to collect the works of earlier writers, just as one collects tools needed in a trade, and he warns against bad influences such as those of flatterers in one's early life. The wide-ranging scope of the work especially appealed to later educator-philosophers such as Erasmus. Plutarch's essay was more practical than say Quintilian's work on education, because it took into account the education of the whole man, not simply of the orator. Then, too, the psychological perceptions offered in *The Education of Children* appealed to subsequent educators.[14]

In concluding his regimen for educating the young, Plutarch returns to an edict based on common sense: "Fathers ought above all, by not misbehaving and by doing as they ought to do, to make themselves a manifest example to their children, so that the latter, by looking at their fathers' lives as at a mirror, may be deterred from disgraceful deeds and words" (I. 20. 67). In every instance concerning these ethically oriented essays in the *Moralia,* whether in advising newlyweds, rulers, mourners, or listeners, Plutarch conducts the reader back to the personal responsibility of examining one's life, then mastering the self.

II *Customs*

For many readers, the *Lives* hold a special fascination not only because of the personages who are depicted in their oversize activities but also for the glimpses those lives provide of the cultures and traditions in the background. Appropriate details about whole peoples or minute idiosyncrasies of a renowned figure help provide fleshly substance to those narratives.

We already know that Plutarch made countless notes on subjects as his attention was drawn to them through his readings, travels, conversations, or simply contemplations. Many of these items, large and small, appear both in the *Moralia* and in the *Lives,* either in identical form or somewhat altered. Consequently, one can read the following about Alexander in his *Sayings of Kings and Commanders* (Vol. III. 14. 59) and recognize its double in Plutarch's *Life of Alexander* (Vol. VII. chapter xxxix): "As he was reading a letter from his mother, which contained secret slanders against Antipater, Hephaestion, as usual, was reading it with him. Alexander did not prevent Hephaestion from reading it, but, when he had finished the reading, he took off his ring, and placed the seal on Hephaestion's lips." The episode reveals the intimacy of their friendship and of course bares Alexander's soul for an instant. Why repeat the moment, we might ask. Plutarch's imaginative powers had not failed him, nor had his memory. But the *Sayings* that treated fragments of events and totaled almost two hundred (see Loeb volume III) represented a storehouse of data and details from which Plutarch drew frequently when writing the *Lives.* Other sections of episodes (one cannot legitimately call them essays) derive from the Romans, from the Spartans, from Spartan women, and from ancient customs found in Sparta.

Yet it would be foolhardy for us, from this range in time, to infer Plutarch jotted down such tidbits in preparing for the *Lives* in advance to actually writing them. What is shown, instead, is his continual interest in people, actions, and customs. If later such an item as that quoted above can be appropriately imbedded in another piece of writing and enhance it, then we have a bonus. But even if the bit of insight remains for posterity in its original form within the *Moralia,* then that is equally worthwhile, from Plutarch's point of view. The value of the pieces scarcely is diminished by a non-narrative shape, as long as readers have access to the unique fund of knowledge encapsuled therein. As stated by one researcher, ". . . the *Morals* have great value historically. No other extant writings give so complete and satisfactory a record of custom and thought in the late Greek period." [15]

As we might expect, Plutarch wrote mostly about the customs of peoples he knew relatively well, such as the Greeks, Romans, barbarians, and to a lesser extent Egyptians. Quite representative of his profound interest in the ways of the world are two essays translated as *The Roman Questions* and *The Greek Questions.* Unfortunately, a third companion piece, *The Barbarian Questions,* has been lost to us. In the works which we have, however, we can see Plutarch's keen, inquisitive mind in operation. The format for many, though by no means all, of the *Questions,* both Greek and Roman, is a thought-provoking question which Plutarch then answers by way of several possible replies. In filtering through the alternative responses that he provides, we become aware of Plutarch's probing mind and vast researches.

In *The Roman Questions,* published probably during the final two or three years of the first century A.D., Plutarch undertakes to discuss one hundred and thirteen Roman customs, most of which are religious in nature. From the answers, we can deduce that despite his own self-effacing statement about not knowing much Latin, Plutarch had to have known the writings of Varro, Livy, Cato (the elder), Fenestella, Verrius Flaccus, Ateius Capito, Figulus, Nigidius, Antistius Labeo, and particularly the works of Juba, king of Mauretania, and *Roman Antiquities* by Dionysius of Halicarnassus.[16] One specimen perhaps will suffice to reveal Plutarch's manner in *The Roman Questions.* At the same time we might better see how Shakespeare's handling of the cultural information turns it into a crucial dramatic device in *Coriolanus.* Number 49 of *The Roman Questions* deals with the ancient method of campaigning for office in Rome:

> Why was it the custom for those canvassing for office to do so in the toga without the tunic, as Cato has recorded?

Was it in order that they might not carry money in the folds of their tunic and give bribes?

Or was it rather because they used to judge candidates worthy of office, not by their family nor their wealth nor their repute, but by their wounds and scars? Accordingly that these might be visible to those that encountered them, they used to go down to their canvassing without tunics.

Or were they trying to commend themselves to popular favour by thus humiliating themselves by their scanty attire, even as they do by hand-shaking, personal appeals, and fawning behaviour? (IV. 49. 81)

The Greek Questions are somewhat less ambitious in dimen sions, explaining as they do only fifty-nine matters of Greek customs. Much derives from Aristotle's writings, the subjects often dealing with religious conventions. Number 24, for instance, explains why a certain roast is called an *enknisma* by the Argives as part of a sacrifice to Apollo (IV. 24. 205–7). But other glimpses into ancient Greek ways are to be found concerning commerce and the formation of nicknames. Like an almanac or desk encyclopedia, *The Greek Questions* are not too proud to consider almost any kind of query. Question number 29, to illustrate, focuses on trading procedures:

Who is the "Seller" among the Epidamnians?

The Epidamnians were neighbours of the Illyrians and perceived that such of their citizens as associated with the Illyrians were becoming corrupted; and, since they feared a revolution, they used to select one of the most reputable of their fellow-citizens each year to conduct such commercial dealings and barters. This man visited the barbarians and provided them with a market and an opportunity for all the citizens to display what they had to sell: thus he was called the "Seller." (IV. 29. 211)

Though perhaps of less historical consequence to economists than the illustration just offered, the following brief query about names reveals Plutarch's lifelong fascination with Greek etymology:

Why is it that Argive children in a certain festival call themselves, in jest, "Pear-throwers"?

Is it because the first men that were led down by Inachus from the mountains to the plain lived, as they say, on wild pears? They also say that wild pears were first discovered by the Greeks in the Peloponnesus at a time when that country was still called Apia, wherefore wild pears were named *"apioi."* (IV. 51. 239)

Closely woven into the fabric of Greece were its religious rites and haunts. In many of his dialogues, consequently, Plutarch employed Delphi as the setting. Issues concerning the gods, the oracles, and related matters arise naturally that way from the background of the discussions. Enigmas which remained with the Greeks over centuries became a part of the culture and ultimately found their way into Plutarch's writings. *The E at Delphi* is such a piece (see Loeb volume V). Stradling the methods of the dialogue and the question-answer framework of the *Questions,* this work considers a lesser-known inscription on the temple at Delphi. Here Ammonius, Lamprias (probably Plutarch's brother), Theon, Eustrophus, Nicander, and others join with Plutarch, who attempts to make some sense of the letter "E" carved on the façade along with the more renowned maxims "Know Thyself" and "Avoid Extremes." Eventually coming out of the exchanges at the gathering are seven possibilities for the significance of the "E," all premised on three seminal possible direct meanings: the Greek name for "E" was "EI," a diphthong meaning the number five; "EI" was also a Greek word for "if"; and "EI" was part of the verb "to be," namely "thou art." By employing his etymological interest, Plutarch sparks some stimulating conversation concerning possible meanings. Ironically, however, an answer satisfying all scholars has yet to be found by classicists, who continue to work with the riddle even today.

A similar dialogue considering a Delphic problem is *The Oracles at Delphi No Longer Given in Verse.*[17] The speakers here, Basilocles, Philinus, Theon, Boëthus, Sarapion, Diogenianus, and a few local guides, are touring the monuments at Delphi and talking on random subjects. At first, no single topic emerges, as they talk about famous people, omens in general, and other matters. The central point, however, gradually takes shape when the participants wonder aloud why in earliest times the oracles were delivered in verse form (hexameters, specifically) while later they were given in brief, simple prose. They conclude that the fashion had changed from the more elaborate form to the straightforward. But not everyone is pleased with the more direct pronouncements, just as not everyone can be pleased at any one time, a conclusion enunciated at the end of the dialogue: "But, just as in those days there were people who complained of the obliquity and vagueness of the oracles, so to-day there are people who make an unwarranted indictment against their extreme simplicity" (V. 30. 343–45).

Much more ambitious an undertaking is Plutarch's *Isis and Osiris*, an extended consideration of the most significant deities of Egypt written in a straight narrative form. Further, Plutarch appears here to be trying to connect the Egyptian gods with certain Greek gods, a difficult task since much could only be theorized. He relies principally on constructing a credible logic in his argument when he attempts to draw the affinities.

Because Plutarch tries to cover so much of a thought-provoking nature in this essay, readers find much to intrigue them. Aside from connecting the various national gods by name, he relates a good deal of strictly Egyptian mythology. Plutarch's own religious convictions also enter in, of course, as do his notions on *daemons*, or demigods. Yet, the classical scholar of today will discern certain weaknesses in Plutarch's facts and line of reasoning. He was no genuine Egyptologist, after all, having visited Egypt once for certain and possibly again for a second time. Most of the data he produces, furthermore, was current common knowledge among the better learned. Plutarch's chief sources for the work appear to have been testimony from Egyptian priests (notorious for their biased revelations) and books, especially those by Herodotus, Aelian, and Diodorus Siculus. When, therefore, Plutarch begins by claiming Isis to be a Greek word and that some writers claim her to be the daughter of Hermes or of Prometheus, we must bear in mind that he is convinced of such Greek-Egyptian relationships and is marshaling those legends that would tend to support his view.

In certain long passages, Plutarch does focus on strictly Egyptian customs, and in those sections he is a mine of information. Early in *Isis and Osiris* he speaks of the Egyptian priests and their policies. Their heads were shaven and they wore only linen, because they could permit nothing impure on their persons. Plutarch also examines their eating and drinking habits in detail, momentarily bringing the ancient Egyptian world close to his readers.

The priests, he continues, would not drink water from the Nile River, though they held it in great honor, because it was reputed to cause obesity (V. 5. 15–17); nor originally did they drink wine at all, ". . . thinking it to be the blood of those who had once battled against the gods, and from whom, when they had fallen and had become commingled with the earth, they believed vines to have sprung. This is the reason why drunkenness drives men out of their senses and crazes them, inasmuch as they are then filled with the blood of their forbears" (V. 6. 17). Certain species of fish were eaten by some Egyptians, but priests never ate any fish, holding that the sea derives from purulent matter not of this world, hence not an earthly element but a corrupt one left over from a foreign substance. Pigs were considered unclean by Egyptians, and onions were detested, partly because they grew during the waning of the moon (V. 8. 21).

The most extensive sections in *Isis and Osiris* treat the topics of the title, the major Egyptian deities. Plutarch's accounts collate closely with those found among other ancient historians, suggesting that his sources and resulting notes were as reliable as could be expected where myth was the basis for information. Despite the Sun's having invoked a curse on Rhea to "not give birth to a child in any month or any year," Hermes, who loved her, won small portions of the moon's illumination periods until he had accumulated a total of five days which he intercalated in addition to the 360 days constituting the year. Appropriately called even then the "birthdays of the gods," those five days saw the birth to Rhea of five gods, one each day: Osiris first, Arueris (also called Apollo and Elder Horus), Typhon, Isis, and last Nephthys, sometimes called Finality, Aphrodite, and Victory (V. 12. 33).

Osiris, the superior of the new gods, coupled with Isis; additionally, he immediately showed his benevolent nature by delivering the Egyptians from destitution and their "brutish way of living," showing them the advantages of civilized life, giving them laws, and teaching them to honor the gods (V. 13. 35). From the first Typhon was the enemy of Osiris. Through the stratagem of a beautiful chest constructed to Osiris' size, he tricked the great god into getting into the box, which Typhon instantly sealed. Then, on November 13, Plutarch records, Typhon threw the chest into the river. The horrid deed first was reported by pans and satyrs living near the river, and since then the tale has been central to Egyptian mythology. Isis, crazed with grief, searched the country until she discovered the chest as part of a pillar in the palace of King Malcander. Isis brought back the chest to her home and hid it. Typhon, however, came upon it and this time cut up the body of Osiris into fourteen pieces, scattering them about. Isis again began a pilgrimage to recover the parts, setting up temples at each location where she discovered a portion of her beloved. And the myth continued with Typhon, manifesting evil, continually battling Isis and Osiris' heirs (V. section 15–22), and with Osiris taking on his role as king of the dead.

But Plutarch goes beyond merely relating a story. As a cultural historian and primitive anthropologist, he sees the representational features of a godhead comprised of Isis, Osiris, and Typhon in terms of natural phenomena. On earth, for instance, and particularly for the Egyptians, the cycles of agricultural fertility affected by wet and dry times of the year are involved, Osiris being equated with the Nile and moisture, and Typhon standing for searing heat which burns off moisture and thus diminishes natural fecundity. Plutarch interprets the process this way:

> The insidious scheming and usurpation of Typhon, then, is the power of drought, which gains control and dissipates the moisture which is the source of the Nile and of its rising . . . and having gained complete mastery, he forces the Nile in retreat to draw back its waters for weakness, and, flowing at the bottom of its almost empty channel, to proceed to the sea. The story told of the shutting up of Osiris in the chest seems to mean nothing else than the vanishing and disappearance of water. (V. 39. 95)

The same Egyptian gods reflect cosmic, as well as earthly, elements, Plutarch continues. According to that doctrine, the gods are forms of the heavenly planets and stars: "There are some who without reservation assert that Osiris is the Sun . . . and there are those who declare that Isis is none other than the Moon. . . . Isis is, in fact, the female principle of Nature, and is receptive of every form of generation . . ." (V. 52/53. 129). For the earthbound reader, Plutarch offers other forms which serve as emblems of Osiris: as an eye and a scepter, "the one of which indicates forethought and the other power" (V. 51. 123), as a keen-eyed hawk who sees all, and indeed anything in "human form of the ithyphallic type" because of his creative powers (V. 51. 125).

The lengthy *Isis and Osiris,* in the last analysis, incorporates countless customs of the Egyptians while tracing their core mytho-religious system. Powers of fecundity and regeneration accrue to Osiris and Isis, who are represented as earth dwellers and heavenly beings. In a section to follow, treating Plutarch's religious writings, we will see how such legendary figures can be accommodated into both worldly and ethereal frameworks by means of his *daemons* theory.

III *Cosmology*

Plutarch's interests extended beyond the human realm into areas of animal behavior and science of all varieties (see Loeb volume XII, which is given over entirely to such topics). Among the most fascinating of his commentaries dealing with science are Plutarch's conjectures about the nonterrestrial universe. In many essays Plutarch alludes to cosmological considerations, usually in passing. The reader of *Isis and Osiris,* it may be remembered, was informally exposed to some of Plutarch's thoughts about the schema of the universe—or stated more exactly, exposed to certain ideas about the moon relatively common to his lettered colleagues. In that essay, Plutarch's chief concern was with some particulars about Egyptian religion. Consequently, glimpses into the cosmos which we are granted come about when he relates universal phenomena with the mythical Egyptian gods:

> There are some who would make the legend an allegorical reference to matters touching eclipses; for the Moon suffers eclipse only when she is full, with the Sun directly opposite to her, and she falls into the shadow of the Earth, as they say Osiris fell into his coffin. Then again, the moon herself obscures the Sun and causes solar eclipses, always on the thirtieth of the month; however, she does not completely annihilate the Sun, and likewise Isis did not annihilate Typhon. (V. 44. 107)

The oblique references to eclipses, as is seen, are brought in simply to amplify his main point about the deities. The same holds true for Plutarch's citing Egyptian priests who say that *daemons* who eventually evolve into full-fledged gods, such as Isis, Osiris, and Typhon, at first pass through an intermediate stage during which "their souls shine as the stars in the firmament" (V. 21. 53).

But in one long article, *Concerning the Face Which Appears in the Orb of the Moon,* Plutarch devotes almost all the discussion to cosmological concerns by concentrating directly on the enigmas of the moon.[18] This animated dialogue includes several knowledgeable participants. Sextus Sulla, Apollonides, Lucius, Theon, Menelaus, possibly Plutarch himself, and Plutarch's brother Lamprias, who serves as leader of the discussions, have gathered ostensibly to hear Sulla's tale as told him by a mysterious stranger. Sulla's myth, however, must wait until the last part of the dialogue, because the men first become engrossed in a consideration of the moon.

Lamprias is the principal spokesman, seeking to answer questions raised about earth's nearest celestial neighbor. He first denies that the moon came into existence vainly, if it was not inhabited; at the same time, however, he adds that there was no compelling reason to believe that a living being could not dwell there. Lamprias' reasons for such confidence paradoxically reveal both a naïveté and a sophistication about the technical exigencies involved. On the one hand, the rotation is gentle, hence "it smooths the air and distributes it in settled order, so that there is no danger of falling and slipping off for those who stand there" (XII. 25. 167); on the other hand, the cold and hot extremes on the moon would tend to temper each other, while the problem of earth in retaining the heat of the sun through its atmosphere would not be applicable to the moon whose "air being tenuous and translucent scatters and diffuses the sun's light, which has no tinder or body to sustain it" (XII. 25. 169).

As for any natural laws on the moon, Lamprias argues that they may well differ from those on earth, so that a form of plant life could exist on the moon without requiring the identical conditions of earth. Similarly, he continues in logical fashion to deduce that a moon being could possess quite different physical characteristics from those of man, in keeping with his environment on his planet (XII. 25. 177). Somewhat playfully, Lamprias suggests to the others that if moon creatures did in fact exist, they probably were viewing the earth with similar mystification: "Those men, I think, would be much more amazed at the earth, when they look out at the sediment and dregs of the universe, as it were, obscurely visible in moisture, mists, and clouds as a lightless, low, and motionless spot, to think that it engenders and nourishes animate beings which partake of motion, breath, and warmth" (XII. 25. 179).

Man always seems to accept strange phenomena more easily when seen as part of a system intelligible to human experience. Plutarch's consideration of the lunar body reflects such a truth. For his spokesmen in this dialogue, the alien planet is at least partly comprehensible as a site for purging man's souls after death. Here, then, cosmography and metaphysics merge: "In the composition of these three factors earth furnishes the body, the moon the soul, and sun furnishes mind [to man] for the purpose of his generation even as it furnishes light to the moon herself. . . . All soul, whether without mind or with it, when it has issued from the body is destined to wander [in] the region between earth and moon but not for an equal time" (XII. 28. 199–201). Hence, during certain eclipses, wails from the processing souls hurry the progress of the moon, especially those cries of the good souls who urge the moon on, "because when they are in the shadow they no longer catch the sound of the harmony of heaven" (XII. 29. 207–9), or what we might call the music of the spheres.

Plutarch offers still another pattern involving the cosmos and long-standing Greek myths when he identifies the Fates with heavenly bodies: "Of the three Fates too Atropos enthroned in the sun initiates generation, Clotho in motion on the moon mingles and binds together, and finally upon the earth Lachesis too puts her hand to the task, she who has the largest share in chance" (XII. 30. 221). And finally, when the speakers turn again to the traditional conundrum concerning the face of the moon, they reveal the common sense found in Plutarch's narratives. They recognize that what appears to be a face is nothing more than gulfs and crevices on the surface of the moon, analogous to the uneven contour of the earth's covering (XII. 29. 209). Plutarch's age, like our own, apparently was willing to contemplate science-fiction possibilities in the universe but not to pursue all theories indiscriminately.

IV *Metaphysics*

Metaphysical issues are so overtly intertwined in Plutarch's writing with morality, customs, and cosmology that we already have encountered many in the essays discussed. Of the basic tenets underlying Plutarch's view of the nonmaterial universal system, two or three stand forth to reveal a philosophy sharing a mutual boundary with religion. Though by no means puritanical in his approach to the needs and pleasures of the body, for example, Plutarch yet insists upon the supremacy of the mind. Plato is his guide in these matters, and Plutarch unhesitatingly adopts entire blocks of Platonic reasoning and thought in his own writings. Once Sulla gets the chance to tell his long-awaited tale in *Concerning the Face Which Appears in the Orb of the Moon,* he quotes his stranger informant verbatim. The stranger, meanwhile, repeats much of what Plato wrote in the *Timaeus* concerning the misconception of man as composed only of two parts:

> The reason is that they suppose mind to be somehow part of soul, thus erring no less than those who believe soul to be part of body, for in the same degree as soul is superior to body, so is mind better and more divine than soul. The result of soul [and body commingled is the irrational or the affective factor, whereas of mind and soul] the conjunction produces reason; and of these the former is source of pleasure and pain, the latter of virtue and vice. (XII. 28. 197)

The centrality of reason here is obvious, just as it was in the *Lives* and in the essays from the *Moralia* already considered. Thus it is that the abode of good sense, the mind, always is found at the apex in Plutarch's scheme. And where the mind is denigrated or subordinated in any fashion, as in Epicurean thought, Plutarch is prompt to inveigh against the violators. Possibly the best example both of his enthroning mind and reason and his attacking opposing beliefs is Plutarch's *That Epicurus Actually Makes a Pleasant Life Impossible.*[19] Plutarch's version of Epicurean thought in this dialogue is brusquely enunciated by Theon, who states of the Epicureans: "They believe that the good is found in the belly and all other passages of the flesh through which pleasure and non-pain make their entrance, and that all the notable and brilliant inventions of civilization were devised for this belly-centered pleasure and for the good expectation of this pleasure" (XIV. 3. 23). Put forth as the correct approach to pleasure and the good life is that which offers delight to the mind instead, in a paraphrase of Plato's doctrines: "But what properly deserves to be considered 'animation' and 'delight' is pure of any taint of its opposite, has no aching or stabbing pain, and brings with it no regret; the good in it is proper to the mind and really 'mental' and authentic and not adventitious or irrational but rational in the truest sense, since it comes from the speculative and philosophical or else the active and honourable part of the mind" (XIV. 9. 57).

Showing through in Plutarch's writings is his personal inclination toward monotheism which in his case appears to be a logical projection of the Olympain hierarchy with Zeus ultimately supreme. There are first principles and laws of Reason governing the universe to which Plutarch holds. In still another dialogue, *The Obsolescence of Oracles,* Plutarch's *raisonneur* again is Lamprias, who ostensibly is responding to the Stoics' alarm about possible multiple worlds. Emerging instead, however, is the faith built on a firm secular-religious conviction:

> . . . what is the need that there be many gods bearing the name of Zeus, if there be more worlds than one, and that there should not be in each world, as pre-eminent governor and ruler of the whole, a god possessing sense and reason, such as the one who among us bears the name of Lord and Father of all? Or again, what shall prevent all worlds from being subject to the Destiny and providence of Zeus, and what shall prevent his overseeing and directing them all in turn and supplying them all with first principles, material sources, and schemes of all that is being carried out? (V. 29. 435)

Plutarch clearly places total credence in all-powerful, all-knowing god. When a crucial metaphysical problem, such as that dealing with divine justice, evokes skepticism in some who (like Job in the Bible) cannot see the grand design in its entirety, Plutarch must defend his supreme deity. *On the Delays of the Divine Vengeance* is such a defense, and one, we should add, that is greatly admired among Plutarch's more philosophically oriented essays. Christian scholars especially find sentiments there close to the Christian doctrine. The dialogue format allows an effective give-and-take situation when Olympicus, Plutarch's son-in-law Patrocleas, and his brother Timon express uneasiness that a man's evil deeds on earth are not promptly punished by divine authority. Their general position is that, if time is permitted to intervene between the bad act and the punishment, the connection of evil rewarded with hurt is lost with the result that no one any longer will fear consequences for doing ill (VII. 3. 189).

The arguments offered by Plutarch to prove that all is for the better in the long run also reveal how deeply rooted those convictions are in him. For example, the blend of religious faith with trust in man's rational powers results in his arguing that proper justice cannot be administered immediately after the deed: ". . . reason . . . acts with justice and moderation only after putting rage and anger out of the way" (VII. 5. 197). Nor would the guilty person have the time to do penance or redeem himself through good acts if he were harshly condemned at once. Again, this displays a consideration on the part of god (VII. 6. 199). Furthermore, there is a fit time and manner for divine punishments. Nor should we forget that sin contains its own reward, in that it "engenders with itself its pain and punishment" (VII. 9. 215).

Hardest to answer for Plutarch is the view that the children need be punished for the offenses of their parents. Timon's point casts doubt on the dealings of god: "For either the actual offenders have been made to pay, and there is no further need to punish the innocent, since even the guilty may not in justice be twice punished for the same offence, or the gods have indolently allowed the punishment of the guilty to lapse, and then, at a late date, exact payment from the innocent, in which case it is not well done to retrieve the tardiness of their punishment by its injustice" (VII. 12. 231). To this Plutarch responds in several ways. First, he denies that all the stories told about illogical and late punishments from the gods are true. Then, he argues empirically that, in fact, the child does take on many of the attributes of the parent, including proclivity towards good or evil. Hence, if a bad act has been committed by the sire, chances are increased that the offspring will do likewise. Plutarch's conclusion is that the child can be punished as a precautionary, or as a preventative measure (VII. 19. 259–61).

Whether or not a reader is thoroughly convinced by these points, it does become obvious that, for Plutarch, god or the gods (he does not remain strictly monotheistic in his phrasing throughout his writing) cannot be guilty of ill deeds. And partly to take into account the evil that does exist in the world, Plutarch develops his concept of *daemons.* In *The Obsolescence of Oracles* he broaches the topic in arguing against a harshness sometimes attributed to the gods. He denounces the notion, for instance, that the gods are bloodthirsty: "Nor is it credible that the gods demanded or welcomed the human sacrifices of ancient days . . ." (V. 14. 391). Instead of assigning ignoble acts to the gods, one should indict the demigods, those beings who stand above man but below the gods: "As for the various tales of rapine and wanderings of the gods, their concealments and banishment and servitude, which men rehearse in legend and in song, all of these are, in fact, not things that were done to the gods or happened to them, but to the demigods . . ." (V. 15. 393). Even when the actual names of the gods are used in describing untoward behavior, we are to understand that it is the *daemons* who perform the deeds, ". . . for each of them is wont to be called after that god with whom he is allied and from whom he has derived his portion of power and honour" (V. 21. 413).[20]

The most complete coverage of the role and evolution of demigods appears in *Isis and Osiris*. As before with an unnamed supreme being, indecorous conduct cannot logically be attributed to Isis, Osiris, and Typhon, if they are to be considered true gods, Plutarch's original premise in discussing Egyptian deities. To remove the onus from such heavenly beings, Plutarch introduces the *daemons* who are to be held responsible: "Better, therefore, is the judgement of those who hold that the stories about Typhon, Osiris, and Isis are records of experiences of neither gods nor men, but of demigods . . ." (V. 25. 59). Plutarch continues this line of thinking by mentioning that Plato, Pythagoras, Homer, Empedocles, Hesiod, Xenocrates, and Chrysippus all speak of such creatures exceeding the human being in powers but more limited than the gods. With Isis and Osiris, there is an added dimension, because at first they truly were demigods. But through their correct conduct, they earned their way ultimately into becoming full-fledged gods: "She herself and Osiris, translated for their virtues from good demigods into gods, as were Heracles and Dionysus later, not incongruously enjoy double honours, both those of gods and those of demigods, and their powers extend everywhere . . ." (V. 27. 67). Yet evil remains in the world and must be accounted for. Typhon epitomized that enervating influence in the Egyptian schema, writes Plutarch, for he continued to enter into combat with the good forces of Osiris and Isis even though they had become deified and he had not. Plutarch leaves matters somewhat unclear in restating the continuing balance in the world between good and evil: "Now Osiris and Isis changed from good minor deities into gods. But the power of Typhon, weakened and crushed, but still fighting and struggling against extinction, they try to console and mollify by certain sacrifices . . ." (V. 30. 73).

What remains puzzling in Plutarch's *daemon* theory is how any forces of evil, such as Typhon, can withstand the supreme power of the good gods. Clearly, evil shows itself on earth, and Plutarch apparently felt obliged to provide it with some metaphysical framework as partial justification. Such unreconciled features of ancient views of the world are understandable in light of the extremely eclectic character of the ethics and metaphysics being constructed during Plutarch's age. As one scholar has pointed out concerning Greek thought of the first century A.D., "The ethical ideal was subject to theological, rational, natural, individual and universal impulses, in the midst of which there existed, with divided authority, a hierarchy of faith and a sovereignty of reason. . . ."[21]

V *Random Concerns*

Naturally, it is unfair to lump together a few additional essays under the indefinite caption "Random Concerns." But there is no other title available that will suggest the immense variety of topics Plutarch brings into play in his *Moralia.* Only a scanning of the essay titles can in any way intimate the multifarious quality of the pieces. Matters of love are considered in several essays, as are issues of political science, domestic customs, and medicine. The *Table-Talk* sections found in volumes VIII and IX of the Loeb editions, for example, abound in commentaries anchored to no specific subject. But as their title indicates, the conversations were to have arisen casually around the dinner table, after the main meal. Of special interest to many readers, nonetheless, are several different essays and dialogues which include esthetics criticism wherein Plutarch reveals himself a conservative judge of the arts.

Plutarch is particularly chary of poetry and music. To round out our look at the *Moralia,* we shall focus on this last subject, for reasons readily comprehended by readers of his other writings. To begin, he values art forms to the extent that they can be applied usefully to instructing men ethically. And when literary accounts tend to obfuscate rather than illuminate certain truths, he flares up in anger, as he does in *Isis and Osiris* in rejecting the fabulous but misleading versions of the lives of the Egyptian gods (V. 20.

49–51). Underlying Plutarch's general animosity toward the arts is his fear that their allure too easily can seduce man's rational powers, leaving him victim to his passions which may be aroused.

The most extensive treatment of the issue arises in his overtly didactic essay *How the Young Man Should Study Poetry.* Plutarch wisely does not advocate a rigorous system of censorship that would forbid youths from being exposed to the siren-like attraction of poetry. Rather, he will trust in an enlightened criterion for judging verse properly:

> Shall we then stop the ears of the young, as those of the Ithacans were stopped, with a hard and unyielding wax, and force them to put to sea in the Epicurean boat, and avoid poetry and steer their course clear of it; or rather shall we set them against some upright standard of reason and there bind them fast, guiding and guarding their judgement, that it may not be carried away from the course by pleasure towards that which will do them hurt? (I. 1. 79)

Plutarch supports his stand that poetry can profitably be read and studied on two seminal premises: verse can help lead the young reader into a fuller understanding of philosophy, and it can provide suitable models of virtue to be emulated in the life of the reader. In the first instance, poetry is viewed as a preface to those philosophical concerns where matters of pleasure and good are involved, just as in poetry: "Wherefore poetry should not be avoided by those who are intending to pursue philosophy, but they should use poetry as an introductory exercise in philosophy, by training themselves habitually to seek the profitable in what gives pleasure, and to find satisfaction therein; and if there be nothing profitable, to combat such poetry and be dissatisfied with it" (I. 1. 81).

Plutarch is equally utilitarian (and candid) regarding the second value of poetry as model. Always a supporter of Homer, he acknowledges that the depictions of courageous deeds in the *Iliad* can indeed inflame the reader to attempt similar good acts. Probably he felt the same about his own *Lives* wherein laudable actions were shown: "For to observe that the most wise and prudent man, when he is in danger of being destroyed and lost, together with the whole host, fears shame and disapprobation, but not death, will make the young man keenly alive to the moral virtues"

(I. 11. 161). But, always a supporter of Plato, Plutarch is conscious of the harm possible in the nontruths promulgated in verse. Hence, he is ever cautioning the young scholar against accepting as necessarily true that information found in poetry (I. 2. 83, and 4. 99).

One other bit of Plutarch's writing reflects his literary criticism as it applies to two great comic playwrights. The *Summary of a Comparison Between Aristophanes and Menander*, though only partial in the form left us, shows the same caution in literary matters that can be seen in his theories. What is particularly revealing in these few pages is the fundamental criterion implied in Plutarch's comments. Old comedy (of approximately the fifth century B.C. in Greece) is best represented by Aristophanes with his brilliant wit, shameless ribaldry, strong invective, and overt iconoclasm. The indecorous, if not the indecent, is fair game in his works. For Plutarch, it is precisely these characteristics of knocking down and ridiculing man's behavior that he finds disgusting, or more accurately degrading. Man, so full of potential when he follows the dictates of good reason, is displayed in Aristophanes' satiric portrayals with blemishes exaggerated and thrust forward. Plutarch's announced world of universal order is thus violated cruelly, in Aristophanes, resulting in harsh condemnation from our moralist:

> But the witticisms of Aristophanes are bitter and rough and possess a sharpness which wounds and bites. And I do not know wherein his vaunted cleverness resides, whether in his words or his characters. Certainly even whatever he imitates he makes worse; for with him roguishness is not urbane but malicious, rusticity not simple but silly, facetiousness not playful but ridiculous, and love not joyous but licentious. (X. 4. 471–73)

There is little in Aristophanes that Plutarch would recommend to the young. The scurrility of the poet's writing would appeal only to the uneducated or emotionally immature young people, which is part of Plutarch's fear, of course. Moreover, Plutarch complains that esthetically, as well as ethically, Aristophanes' plays were indecorous: ". . . in his diction there are tragic, comic, pompous, and prosaic elements, obscurity, vagueness, dignity, and elevation, loquacity and sickening nonsense. And with all these differences and dissimilarities his use of words does not give to each kind its fitting and appropriate use . . ." (X. 1. 467).

Menander is different in Plutarch's estimation. The perfect playwright representative of new comedy of the fourth century B.C., Menander steered clear of political matters of personal charges in his plays. His works concentrated on reflecting the life of his day, which resulted in polished comedies of character wherein items indecent at all were conveyed through innuendo rather than through bold grossness. For Plutarch, Menander was much more dependable than Aristophanes. In the matter of artistic decorum, for example, Menander's diction fitted the characterizations in a realistic rather than caricaturistic fashion. As Plutarch states, "But Menander's diction is . . . polished and its ingredients mingled into . . . [a] consistent . . . whole" (X. 2. 467). Clearest of all the criteria involved in Plutarch's evaluation of the two dramatists is the didactic factor, and in that area Menander wins handily: "Now Aristophanes is neither pleasing to the many nor endurable to the thoughtful. . . . But Menander, along with his charm, shows himself above all satisfying. He has made his poetry, of all the beautiful works Greece has produced, the most generally accepted subject in theatres, in discussions, and at banquets, for readings, for instruction, and for dramatic competition" (X. 3. 469).

Woven throughout Plutarch's specific commentaries and his offhand remarks are verdicts on the arts, suggesting a definite utilitarian attitude. Every form of art has a proper function, usually didactic, which becomes its reason for being. Art for art's sake is a totally alien concept for Plutarch. Thus, though he displays an active interest in such issues as musical harmonics (see his *Table-Talk,* VII, VIII, and IX), he also writes from a prescriptive point of view regarding art, as he does, for example, in Question 8 from *Table-Talk* VII, "What kinds of entertainment are most appropriate at dinner," and in Question 1 from *Table-Talk* IX, "On opportune and inopportune quotations from the poets." One does not separate art forms from life itself in Plutarch's mind; one thing influences everything else.

Music, to take one last illustration, does not remain a simple trifle. Plutarch recognizes it as a potentially enervating force, especially where the passions of man are concerned. Therefore, it must be seen as possibly subversive to man's reasoning powers and consequently needs to be regulated. In Question 5 from *Table-Talk* VII, "That one should guard especially against the pleasures derived from degenerate music, and how to do so," he opens by recounting a dinner he attended at which a skilled musician performed for the entertainment of the guests:

And for a fact it was a fine performance to hear—at first. But then, shaking the hall and filling it with resounding noise, when he perceived that most of the auditors were so overwhelmed as to allow him, under the spell of pleasure, to do with them what he pleased and hypnotize them with his piping or even with licentious movements, he cast off all disguise and showed that music can inebriate, more effectively than any wine, those who drink it in as it comes, with no restraint. (IX. 1. 43)[22]

The perils are clear when the senses are assaulted with sensations of pleasure, all of which can lead to deterioration of man's Reason. In the dialogue, Plutarch permits his brother Lamprias to isolate the pertinent facts for the others in attendance, who are oblivious to the consequences of the alluring music: " 'Hence we must be especially wary of these pleasures; they are extremely powerful, because they do not, like those of taste and touch and smell, have their only effect in the irrational and "natural" part of our mind, but lay hold of our faculty of judgement and prudence' " (IX. 3. 51–53).

Once again, as in his essay *How the Young Man Should Study Poetry,* Plutarch eschews the remedy of the narrow-minded moralist. To forbid listening to music, just as to outlaw reading of poetry, is not the solution. Instead, Plutarch returns to his humanistic axis to propose that the antidote for debilitating music arises from exposing the hearer to more proper music. Man's reason then will evaluate the two forms and effect the correct choice in the person: ". . . but it is possible to take a man who is enjoying mimes and tunes and lyrics that are bad art and bad taste, and lead him back to Euripides and Pindar and Menander . . ." (IX. 4. 55). Faith in man's essential capacity to identify the good from the bad and act accordingly thus turns Plutarch away from an absolute stance inimical to the arts.

CHAPTER 5

Plutarch's Thought Crystallized

EVEN Plutarch's most ardent supporters concur that the enlightened Greek who was so instrumental in transmitting much of the ancient world down the ages did not himself create any new philosophical system. Most readers of Plutarch today would agree that little of a probing nature is involved; rather, it is a restatement of the thinking then current.[1] At the same time, as we shall be observing in the following chapter, Plutarch's writings proved to inspire many of the most influential writers and thinkers of later years. Thus, it was his fate to furnish the proper soil which permitted the crops of later generations to flourish.

Notwithstanding the absence of a powerful originality of mind in Plutarch, it is amply clear that he held to certain primary beliefs. Specifically, his faith in a cosmic order that was not always readily discernible informs all that he wrote, and it is that trust in a universal law which remains ever-present as a backdrop to what he wrote. Because of the proximity in time of Plutarch's life span to that of Christ, attempts have been made to align his religious inclinations with Christianity, especially in light of certain affinities, such as humaneness, adamant faith in a supreme power, and the perpetuation of souls after death. That connection never has been made on the basis of credible proof of any sort: not one authority in the classical field has claimed conclusive evidence which would link Plutarch and Christ.[2] We are left to conclude that Plutarch's faith was a pagan one with respect to Christianity, but one which was deistic. Stemming from his belief in a universal force was Plutarch's strong didactic sense: man must lead his life in accordance with the larger scheme engineered by the metaphysical essence. Cosmic order, then, had to be translated to the earthly setting to provide guidance in men's lives. Plutarch's self-assumed role in everything he wrote was to reveal the larger plan and to urge his fellow mortals to attain the parallel worldly harmony. R. H. Barrow sums up the case in this fashion: "Men like Plutarch, and Plutarch pre-eminently, felt themselves charged with a mission to make known the ideal and achievements and experience of the past, believing sincerely that in them the men of their day would find satisfaction as they sought new springs of inspiration for their lives and new standards of thought and action." [3]

Plutarch's limitless faith shines forth as an urgent humanism. Man's personal conduct and professional actions are all to be founded on the bedrock of humanism, on trust in man's rational powers. For that reason, whatever discussion is being pursued in Plutarch's writings, the notion of reason appears sooner or later. In politics, for example, the humanistic doctrines of moderation and self-knowledge are introduced repeatedly, even as they are in the distant area of the arts. In the present chapter, we shall be viewing those concepts of Plutarch which are most often reiterated in his writing and which therefore disclose the focal points of his thoughts.

I *Plutarch's Consciousness of Deity*

Both in his *Lives* and the *Moralia*, Plutarch shows great respect for divinity. The short essay *Superstition*, from the *Moralia* (LCL, volume II), is his way of revealing the greater dangers inherent in superstition even compared to those in atheism, though he openly disavows both. Atheism, he suggests, can well lead man into a depleting indifference because he cannot fear godly power, since he does not believe in gods. Superstition, on the other hand, is much more enervating because the superstitious person dreads the divinity to an extent that "utterly humbles and crushes a man," all because he associates the divine power with "the cause of pain and injury" (II. 2. 457). However, Plutarch will not endorse atheism, which he sees as an ignorance in man leading to great misfortune, "for it is as if the soul had suffered the extinction of the brightest and most dominant of its many eyes, the conception of God" (II. 5. 467).

The precise nature of Plutarch's divine being is impossible to ascertain. On the basis of his many remarks concerning the Creator, we can say that he leans toward the concept of one god, despite the common use of the term "gods" when speaking of religious issues (a fact we noted in the previous chapter). H. J. Rose's observation concerning Plutarch's religio-moral stance comes closest to describing the situation: "With these ethics goes a religion which may be described as a philosophical monotheism with loopholes for polytheism. As with so many Greek writers, it makes very little difference whether Plutarch says 'God' or 'the divine' . . . or 'the gods,' when speaking of such things as the moral government of the universe." [4] Plutarch's own most definite assertion in this connection appears in that rich storehouse *Isis and Osiris* from the *Moralia* (LCL volume V). Behind the specific material he gives there regarding Egyptian deities stands his larger thesis that the essentials of Egyptian religion are the same as those of the Greek. Only the names are sometimes different, continues Plutarch: ". . . just as the sun and the moon and the heavens and the earth and the sea are common to all, but are called by different names by different peoples, so for that one rationality which keeps all these things in order and the one Providence which watches over them and the ancillary powers that are set over all, there have arisen among different peoples, in accordance with their customs, different honours and appellations" (V. 67. 157).

Aside from a fundamental monotheism, Plutarch reveals himself to be a dedicated disciple of Plato, particularly with respect to the notion of a dual material and ideal realm of ideas. Plato, as well as Plutarch, considered God as the ultimate cause for all that happens in the world, just as both writers promulgated the concept of reason and philosophy to be superior in men.[5] At the same time, Plutarch also reflects strong infusions of Aristotelianism. And despite his frequent verbal attacks on Stoicism (with its forbidding determinism), he nonetheless mirrors traces of Stoic doctrines. In the last analysis, one is forced to conclude that Plutarch is informally eclectic in the formation of his philosophical attitudes, ruling out only Epicureanism. As a result, when Archbishop Trench espies strains of orientalism in Plutarch, and Robert Flacelière judges him as representative of "Middle Platonism," such scholars simply isolate a few threads among the many going into his syncretistic philosophical framework.

In an earlier section analyzing the *Moralia*, we commented on Plutarch's employment of the *daemon* theory to account for the evil which obviously exists in the world. As we noted then, the divinity that Plutarch envisions governing the cosmos cannot be guilty of creating wickedness. "The fact is that it is impossible for anything bad whatsoever to be engendered where God is the Author of all" (V. 45. 109) is Plutarch's statement in *Isis and Osiris* (LCL volume V). In that same treatise, we learned of a balance between good and evil, wherein the principle of good is superior (as in Osiris and Isis opposed to Typhon) but unable to rid the world entirely of the evil strain in existence: "Yet it is impossible for the bad to be completely eradicated, since it is innate, in large amounts, in the body and likewise in the soul of the Universe, and is always fighting a hard fight against the better. . . . Typhon is that part of the soul which is impressionable, impulsive, irrational and truculent, and of the bodily part the destructible, diseased and disorderly . . ." (V. 49. 121). When we then see the *daemons* introduced as intermediaries between the perfect plan and the faulty world, we readily comprehend how Plutarch became involved with the theories of Zoroaster, or Zarathustra (see section 46, pages 111–13, of *Isis and Osiris*). The fact that, in introducing the theory of *daemons*, Plutarch was popularizing a highly superstitious doctrine and thus was inconsistent with his attitude toward superstition does not appear to have disturbed him. Plutarch's demigods satisfied a more urgent need in his thinking. As Wilmer C. Wright has stated, the *daemon* hypothesis "was an effort to purify Greek theology and to justify the ways of god to man."[6]

Of equal importance in Plutarch's religious views was his unshakable belief in an afterlife for the soul. The issue perhaps arises most clearly in *On the Delays of the Divine Vengeance* in the *Moralia* (LCL volume VII). There, he has stated the crucial position specifically: "It is one and the same argument, then . . . that establishes both the providence of God and the survival of the human soul, and it is impossible to upset the one contention and let the other stand" (VII. 18. 257). We may recall, moreover, that in Plutarch's metaphysics the souls of men undergo a process of purification once separated from the bodies by death, a concept compatible with similar ones proposed by Plato and Aristotle. The myth eventually repeated in *On the Delays of the Divine Vengeance* tells of the dissolute man of Soli, who was permitted a glimpse of the afterworld when clinging precariously to life, following a near-fatal fall. When Thespesius, the name given to the man during his otherworldly excursion, is escorted among the souls being treated there, he learns that Adrasteia (or "the inescapable"), daughter of Necessity and Zeus, supervises the administration of punishment for all crimes. Assisting her are three wardens and executioners; each is charged with punishing souls according to the seriousness of the misdemeanor. For relatively minor sins, Poinê assigned a corresponding penalty, Dikê (or Justice) for worse errors, and Erinys (or Fury) for the most heinous crimes. Plutarch's description of the various torments connected with the punishment system (VII. 25. 279–85) brings to mind the levels of Hell in Dante's Inferno, particularly when the recompense is an inverted, painful form of the initial sin.

In the *Life of Romulus* (LCL volume I), Plutarch also touched on the subject of the progression of good souls toward a reunion with the godhead, a doctrine which unquestionably followed Plato. When he relates Romulus' extraordinary disappearance, Plutarch slows his narrative to offer commentary concerning such a phenomenon. A man's quite unique soul

> comes from them [i.e., the gods], and to them it returns, not with its body, but only when it is most completely separated and set free from the body, and becomes altogether pure, fleshless, and undefiled. . . . We must not, therefore, violate nature by sending the bodies of good men with their souls to heaven, but implicitly believe that their virtues and their souls, in accordance with nature and divine justice, ascend from men to heroes, from heroes to demi-gods, and from demi-gods, after they have been made pure and holy, as in the final rites of initiation, and have freed themselves from mortality and sense, to gods, not by civic law, but in very truth and according to right reason, thus achieving the fairest and most blessed consummation. (I. 28. 181–83)

The myth told in *On the Delays of Divine Vengeance* concludes with another possibility regarding the processing of dead men's souls: metempsychosis. Not all the souls follow the direct steps toward reunification with god as told in the Romulus account. Transmigration occurs for the spirits of evildoers. In the myth told by the man of Soli, such souls awaiting a second birth are prepared by being hammered, dismantled, welded, and generally shaped into new forms. With a touch of humor, Plutarch has his spokesman comment on finding the soul of Nero among those being worked on. "Already in a sorry plight and pierced with incandescent rivets," Nero's spirit was to have become a viper which purportedly eats its way out of its mother's womb; it will be recalled that Nero had commanded his own mother slain. But a voice projecting from a light altered plans, a voice which stated that Nero should become a "vocal creature," or frog, instead. This was because Nero had considered himself a vocalist and musician. Plutarch then concludes the episode by explaining that Nero's reprieve resulted from his having done one good deed during his lifetime: he emancipated Greece in A.D. 67 (VII. 32. 297–99).

II *The Humanistic Core of Plutarch's Thought*

There is no break in the arc of Plutarch's thinking between attaining the divine and leading the correct life on earth. The two processes are completely integrated, as we have just observed with the concept of reincarnation of souls. The good man on earth is well on his way toward communion with godhead upon the loss of bodily life; the evil man must undergo extensive and painful purgations, including transmigration. While on earth, however, man has been given the supreme faculty of reason, which permits him to avoid sin and do good, if he does not abuse or ignore those rational powers.[7]

All in a single package, therefore, we find in Plutarch's thought elements which are quasi-Platonic, Christian, Oriental, and distinctly humanistic. Such an eclectic approach to metaphysical philosophy is described by T. R. Glover in this way: "This one ultimate Reason is described by Plutarch in terms borrowed from all the great teachers who had spoken to the Greeks of God. The Demiurge, the One and Absolute, the World-Soul and the rest all contribute features." [8] Hence, reason, in Plutarch's scheme, offers man needed guidance during his worldly sojourn, while after death only the soul can make the connection with godhead.[9] Such a total reliance on the resources found in reason is neither new with Plutarch, nor can reason be considered an heroic remedy. Yet, by employing good sense and moderation—humanistic keystones—in daily life, man has the opportunity to formulate his Fate, at least in part. If such were not the case, the alternative for man would be bleak indeed, as Plutarch insists when arguing against any absolute conclusions regarding chance: "Wherefore, if we impute the works of sagacity to chance, let the works of justice and of self-control be also ascribed to chance, and, by Heaven, let thieving, stealing purses, and licentious living all be ascribed to chance, and let us abandon all our reasoning processes and resign ourselves to chance, to be driven and carried, as dust or rubbish by a violent wind, hither and thither" (*Chance* from the *Moralia,* LCL II. 2. 77). The identical sentiment was observable in our second chapter when we examined the comparison of the lives of Theseus and Romulus. Luckily for mankind, however, reason acts as man's skeleton key, opening doors to the good life. Again in the essay *Chance,* Plutarch writes that ". . . man, for all his senses, had he not mind and reason, would not differ at all in his life from the brutes" (II. 3. 79).

Nor is this insistence upon common sense and the self-control which then results depicted as onerous. A happy life as well as a good life accrues to the man utilizing reason in his actions. His most unqualified assertion to that effect comes in *Isis and Osiris* in the *Moralia* (LCL volume V), when he says, "The fact is that nothing of man's usual possessions is more divine than reasoning, especially reasoning about the gods; and nothing has a greater influence toward happiness" (V. 68. 159). Even for those dedicated to indulging the senses to attain happiness, Plutarch's humanistic thesis that reason leads to moderation remained valid. For instance, in the essay *Advice About Keeping Well* (LCL volume II in the *Moralia*), which we looked at in the preceding chapter, Plutarch argued for maintaining good health so that the lover of pleasure could pursue his desired course unimpaired. Fundamentally, all the same, he believed that the pleasures in life derived from one's own being, as he states in *Virtue and Vice* from the *Moralia* (LCL volume II): "But a pleasant and happy life comes not from external things, but, on the contrary, man draws on his own character as a source from which to add the element of pleasure and joy to the things which surround him" (II. 1. 95). Ultimate peace of mind for man, Plutarch continues, springs from the search for the good: "You will be contented with your lot if you learn what the honourable and good is" (II. 4. 101). Such, of course, is the essence of humanistic self-knowledge. Moreover, for Plutarch, the awareness induced through reason permits man to banish the fears associated with the unknown. He remarks in *Life of Solon* (LCL volume I): "For it is weakness, not kindness, that brings men into endless pains and terrors when they are not trained by reason to endure the assaults of fortune" (I. 7. 421).

III *Humanism and the Active Life*

On several occasions during the course of this book, we have commented on the activism constructed within Plutarch's so-called philosophy. Esoteric theories designed to baffle the reader had no part in his purpose. The engaged life, directed toward the good, was his final aim when moralizing; the active life meant becoming involved in civic and religious functions. As Archbishop Trench so cogently worded it, "Plutarch could the less endure this voluntary abdication on men's part of all active share in the world's business, from the strong conviction which he entertained —a conviction, indeed, which seemed inborn to every Greek—of the necessity of public life for the harmonies and full development of the whole circle of the mental and moral faculties. . . ." [10]

His essay entitled *How a Man May Become Aware of His Progress in Virtue* (*Moralia,* LCL volume I) is forthright in requiring a participatory response, for ". . . the translating of our judgements into deeds, and not allowing our words to remain mere words, but to make them into actions, is, above all else, a specific mark of progress" (I. 14. 447–49). It is not surprising that we find ample representation of this particular view of Plutarch in his *Parallel Lives,* where he focuses entirely upon the greatest men of action from the classical past. There, we discover that all the humanistic tenets taught as essential to man's personal well-being apply equally to the bold leader. Plutarch urged, in *To an Uneducated Ruler* (LCL volume X in the *Moralia*), that rulers provide their citizens with model deportment suitable for emulation. Numa, in Plutarch's estimate, proved precisely such an ideal standard for his peoples. As Plutarch writes of the worthy in *Life of Numa* (LCL volume I), "Such a life is the noblest end of all government, and he is most a king who can inculcate such a life and such a disposition in his subjects" (I. 20. 377). The same point was underlined in *Life of Dion* (LCL volume VI) when Dion decided to bring Plato to Sicily so that the character of the king's son "might be regulated by the principles of virtue, and that he might be conformed to that divinest and most beautiful model of all being in obedience to whose direction the universe issues from disorder into order" (X. 21). Furthermore, in the *Life of Aristides* (LCL volume II), Plutarch repeats his seminal doctrine of the necessity for reason in a man's acts, here, with respect to administrating justice: ". . . but in fundamental justice nothing participates except through the exercise of intelligent reasoning powers" (II. 6. 229). Camillus, too, reflects the identical humanism woven throughout Plutarch's *Lives* and *Moralia*. In his instance, ". . . it was his moderation that kept his rule from exciting envy" (*Life of Camillus*, LCL II. 197).

Countless additional specimens of Plutarch's central doctrines stud his accounts of the lives of grand noblemen, and they need not be considered again here. But what is reinforced by scanning the *Lives*, after viewing Plutarch's fundamental beliefs in the abstract, is that the finest rulers from antiquity were those coming closest to the humanistic notions regarding life. When a hero slips from prominence, it almost always is because of a misstep caused by immoderation or irrationality. In the last analysis, no good can stem from anything which does not contain God, and God's will is possible only when man engages reason in his life.

IV *Plutarch's Political Views*

Exactly where Plutarch stood with regard to the various forms of political systems with which he was acquainted is not absolutely clear. Nor have other scholars of our sage, writing about his activities at Chaeronea, been of much assistance. J. and W. Langhorne, to illustrate, state without hesitation that "with regard to Plutarch's political principles, it is clear that he was, even whilst at Rome, a republican in heart, and a friend to liberty. . . . At Chaeronea we find him more openly avowing the principle of liberty."[11] That view, however, is not held by everyone. The classicist J. P. Mahaffy reports with equal confidence that Plutarch "regarded the lowering of the franchise to include free paupers as idle and mischievous. He thinks that monarchy is ideally the most perfect state." [12] Neither observer is wholly accurate, for Plutarch nowhere suggests that one form of governing is ideal in every way for any given age. Each absolute system has its built-in drawbacks. As with other areas in Plutarch's conceptions, we are left with the impression that he personally preferred some intermediate structure which held two or more separate systems in balance. Political scientists call it the theory of mixed politics. First, however, we need to examine the information Plutarch did make available.

The fragmentary essay called *On Monarchy, Democracy, and Oligarchy* from the *Moralia* (LCL volume X) is disappointing to the reader approaching it for a look at Plutarch's political opinions. Its extreme brevity warns the reader in advance that not a great deal could be covered there in depth. Moreover, even its attribution to Plutarch has become suspect in recent times. But if Plutarch did not write the original piece, whoever did (possibly a student of his, as is believed true of some other essays gathered with those known to be Plutarch's) offers conservative views resembling Plutarch's. When, therefore, the author analyzes the nature of three forms of government which had succeeded about that time, he only points out what any casual observer of history would recognize as true: Whenever absolute monarchy, aristocratic oligarchy, and self-governing democracy miss the mark, their perversions breed violence, arrogance, "anarchy, equality, excess, and all of them folly" (X. 3. 309). If one were to choose among the various forms of government, writes the unknown author, then the selection of monarchy would make the best sense, since only thereby can virtue be sustained at a high peak, just as Plato had written. The determinant offered is based on the underlying strength and weakness within a system such as democracy especially: "For the other forms of government in a certain sense, although controlled by the statesman, control him, and although carried along by him, carry him along, since he has no firmly established strength to oppose those from whom his strength is derived . . ." (X. 4. 311).

Such a view, pointing out the limited powers left to a ruler in the more self-determining systems, mirrors statements known to be Plutarch's own. In *Precepts of Statecraft* (*Moralia,* volume X in LCL) he teaches a doctrine of gradually taking complete charge of the people by means of careful and conscious psychology: "But for the statesman it is fitting, not to imitate the character of his people, but to understand it and to employ for each type those means by which it can be brought under his control" (X. 3. 167–69). Readers hoping to discover statements in Plutarch expressly favoring the democratic construct in government will be disappointed. Perhaps the theory of democracy is not disagreeable to Plutarch; but from his didactic, paternalistic bias, he pragmatically discerns the inherent possibilities for trouble. His advice about the state requires that "at the base of political activity there must be a firm and strong foundation, a choice of policy arising from judgement and reason . . ." (X. 2. 159–61). Yet, he continues, for whatever reasons (and he proposes several, as is his pattern) the people of democracies "make use of those who happen to turn up" in selecting their representatives, and they are just as casual about dismissing those leaders when they have become wearied with them (X. 4. 173). Finally, because so much of leading stems from the ruler's personality and ability to make speeches (the equivalent, of course, to our modern political image syndrome) the masses are particularly susceptible to appeals to the emotions: "For leadership of a people is leadership of those who are persuaded by speech; but enticing the mob . . . is exactly like catching and herding irrational beasts" (X. 5. 181).

Probably the most outspoken instance treating the perils of citizen power in the state is the *Life of Coriolanus* (LCL volume IV). Plutarch there relates the fortunes of a leader whose bias in favor of the aristocracy is never concealed. All the same, the fervor and effectiveness of Coriolanus' arguments against the witless rabble suggest that Plutarch found such lines of logic not unlike his own. Coriolanus' plea to the senate, for example, that Rome not freely distribute grains to the citizenry who were in want, derives from a rational proposition: to reward the very workers who had caused the hardship in the first place would only invite further illogical concessions at a later time. His case began, of course, with the additional power given to the tribunate, which he viewed as diluting the authority of the senate itself. Also, the people as a result began to refuse to obey their consuls. At first Plutarch paraphrases the harangue of Coriolanus before the senate, saying: "To sit there . . . voting such a people largesses and supplies, like those Greeks where democracy is most extreme, he said was nothing more nor less than maintaining them in their disobedience . . ." (XVI. 155). But as the speech of Coriolanus gains in intensity, Plutarch quotes him directly, including some very persuasive rationale:

For they surely will not say that they are getting those as a grateful return for the military services which they omitted, and the secessions by which they renounced their country, and the calumnies against the senate which they have countenanced. They will rather be confident that your fears drive you to subserviency and flattery when you make them these gifts and concessions, and will set no limit to their disobedience, nor cease from their quarrels and seditions. Such action on our part would therefore be sheer madness. . . . (XVI. 157)

These arguments are powerful and their logic is basically sound. But that does not mean Plutarch necessarily favors an absolute monarchy. In fact, he warns against the tyrant, a role easily played by an absolute king.[13] At the same time, Plutarch lauds Alexander's accomplishing what Zeno had only written about in the *Republic:* the blending of different peoples within "one community and one polity" wherein all could "consider as their fatherland the whole inhabited earth" (*On the Fortune or the Virtue of Alexander*, in volume IV of LCL *Moralia,* part one, 6. 397–99).

After he considers the alternatives, neither the autocratic policies of the unchallenged monarch-tyrant nor the fickle decisions or the mass rule under democracy wins Plutarch's clear-cut endorsement. In the *Lives* the ruins of grand states are strewn without consideration of nationality. Earning Plutarch's highest praise, however, is Lycurgus' Sparta, whose policies, as we noted in our second chapter, remained workable and hence unchanged for five hundred years. In the final analysis, it is one's definition of the ends of a commonwealth that determines which structure most nearly succeeds. With respect to Sparta, Plutarch is explicit about Lycurgus' goal: "It was not, however, the chief design of Lycurgus then to leave his city in command over a great many others, but he thought that the happiness of an entire city, like that of a single individual, depended on the prevalence of virtue and concord within its own borders. The aim, therefore, of all his arrangements and adjustments was to make his people free-minded, self-sufficing, and moderate in all their ways, and to keep them so as long as possible" (I. 31. 301, *Life of Lycurgus,* LCL volume I). Such an end should be the desire of any ruler, writes Plutarch in *Precepts of Statecraft,* when asserting that the "greatest blessings which States can enjoy" are "peace, liberty, plenty, abundance of men, and concord" (X. 32. 291). Plutarch argues for Alexander on identical grounds in *On the Fortune or the Virtue of Alexander.* He defends the King's excursions into Asia on the basis of Alexander's desire "to render all upon earth subject to one law of reason and one form of government and to reveal all men as one people." Like Lycurgus, Plutarch avers, Alexander operated according to an altruistic intent: ". . . the very plan and design of Alexander's expedition commends the man as a philosopher in his purpose not to win for himself luxury and extravagant living, but to win for all men concord and peace and community of interests" (IV. 8, 9. 405).

To attain harmony in Sparta, Lycurgus (apparently Plutarch's supreme lawgiver) made several significant alterations in the governmental operations of the state. The first and most crucial change, Plutarch emphasizes, was his establishment of the senate which would force the monarch to share his powers with the people. Although Werner Jaeger may be right in considering Plutarch a romanticist when glamorizing the accomplishments effected by Lycurgus' emendations in the state, the logic behind the changes is persuasive.[14] The notion of a shifting middle factor which could keep the political extremes in check (and hence balanced) is expressed by Plutarch in his *Life of Lycurgus:*

For before this the civil polity was veering and unsteady, inclining at one time to follow the kings toward tyranny, and at another to follow the multitude towards democracy; but now, by making the power of the senate a sort of ballast for the ship of state and putting her on a steady keel, it achieved the safest and the most orderly arrangement, since the twenty-eight senators always took the side of the kings when it was a question of curbing democracy, and, on the other hand, always strengthened the people to withstand the encroachments of tyranny. (I. 5. 221)

Whether or not we feel that Plutarch was justified in honoring the feats of Lycurgus in blueprinting a governmental pattern, political theorists do remain impressed. As Z. S. Fink comments, ". . . what is notable about it [i.e., Lycurgus' arrangement] is the suggestion that the stability of mixed polities arose from the fact that what we may call the middle element held the balance *between* the other two. Of both this idea and the older notion of the three elements checking one another, much in later times was to be heard." [15]

In attempting to establish a steady position for Plutarch with respect to political systems, we become aware that he is no more a purist in this connection than he is in religion or philosophy. When he speaks of liberty for the people of a state, he apparently does not intend them to have a democracy. We learned our lesson on that point from Plutarch's "Comparison of Lycurgus and Numa" (LCL volume I in the *Lives*); there, Numa's more self-governed land is passed over in favor of Lycurgus' stringent guidelines for running the state. More often than not, in Plutarch's accounts of rule by great men, an autocratic arrangement works out more expediently, at least as far as the final accomplishments of the state are concerned. If we ultimately are left with the impression that some type of monarchy would be acceptable to Plutarch, we are sensing in part the general drift of his age which more and more favored strict monarchies. Our understanding of such a phenomenon is all the easier to come by if T. A. Sinclair's observations are trustworthy concerning growing religious basis for autocratic rule: "The more absolute the power of the Roman emperor became, the stronger became the connection between monotheism and monarchy. It appeared to be self-evident that, as there was but one supreme ruler on earth and one sun in the sky, the same must also be true of Heaven and of the whole Universe; it was felt that the virtues of a good ruler were none other than the attributes of God." [16] Such an orderly parallel would have appealed to Plutarch.

V *Plutarch's Views of the Arts*

Most of Plutarch's direct statements concerning the arts are to be found in the *Moralia*. For that reason we commented on the general issue of his opinions in that area as part of the preceding chapter. What we can add here, then, becomes a postscript, bringing into account Plutarch's occasional allusions to the arts in the *Lives*, as well as recent scholarly observations concerning Plutarch's esthetics.

There is a clear priority in life, according to everything that Plutarch set down in writing. Philosophy, or ethics, always stood at the apex of his hierarchy, as we have observed repeatedly. When it came to the arts, there arose no question: all art forms must be viewed as subordinate to moral values. To turn again to the *Life of Lycurgus*, we can recall the pleased tone of Plutarch as he relates how Lycurgus banished "the unnecessary and superfluous arts" (I. 9. 231). Equally illuminating is Plutarch's *Life of*

Solon (LCL volume I), in which he tells an episode from Solon's later life which concerns the renowned Thespis. When Solon was rather old, Plutarch relates, he went to see Thespis, who at that time was beginning to develop the tragic form in drama. Following the performance, Solon heatedly reproached Thespis for telling lies before the audience, a charge which Thespis shunted aside since no harm could come from it within the limits of a play. Solon, however, would not be appeased and replied in anger, "Soon, however, if we give play of this sort so much praise and honour, we shall find it in our solemn contracts" (I. 29. 489). What is shown by the tale is that Plutarch considered poetry a form of untruth, since it spoke of things which did not take place in actual life.[17]

We come face to face with an anomaly on this issue, because Plutarch was well read for his time. "In fact, Plutarch was both a literary and an art critic, and, in the best sense of the word, an antiquarian. He had a wide familiarity with all the poets and prose writers of Greece and was also interested in works of art, inscriptions and numismatics," concludes the French classicist Robert Flacelière.[18] Despite his learning and natural inquisitiveness regarding man's capacities in life, Plutarch still could not place a high value on what we call the creative arts. His moral sense was violated by the element of deception that he sensed in poetry and drama, for example. Part of the reason no doubt stems from the artist's intent to "please or amaze the audience," which in Plutarch's mind meant attempting to divert man's rational senses by way of the emotions.[19] For the same reason, Plutarch has been found wanting as an accurate observer of the theater of his day or as conveyor of earlier descriptions of drama.[20] Readers of Plato will recognize the same symptoms of suspicion of literature as such and its down-grading, a fact well examined in Jaeger's *Paideia.* In Plutarch, too, the centrality of life is philosophy, particularly moral philosophy, leaving poetry only as its bridesmaid.

CHAPTER 6

The Influence and Significance of Plutarch

TO comprehend the depth of Plutarch's significance is to grasp the scope of his influence. Merely to assert, as does one eminent classicist, that Plutarch "is simply one of the most influential writers who ever lived" just scratches the surface of the issue.[1] In Plutarch's case, we have an instance of intellectual and literary transmission on an enormous scale, extending beyond geographic and time boundaries to make his writings viable even today. Additionally, as we undertake the task of sketching in the effect of Plutarch on men writing long after his lifetime, we must be conscious that by necessity we are dealing principally with influences of a direct nature, those readily felt and discerned. Meanwhile, the indirect consequences of Plutarch's work may never surface sufficiently for the casual observer to detect them. We can only conjecture in the latter instance, suggesting that this writer or that thinker was expressing a Plutarchian concept in transmuted form. All the same, we ultimately should bear in mind that Plutarch himself adopted and adapted the materials which traversed his intellectual path. If we are guilty of oversight in attributing to our Sage of Chaeronea what rightly should be his, we might draw comfort in recalling that Plutarch himself was borrowing from predecessors, some of whom slipped from sight in the process of their transmutation through him.

Before he could be useful to later generations, Plutarch had to be available and read by others. In manuscript form he was known to most learned scholars even during the darkest days of the Middle Ages. The full impact of the information he perpetuated, however, was not to be felt until later. In paradigmatical fashion, Plutarch rode the crest of humanistic learning during Europe's Renaissance to awaken the Western world to paramount features of the past. Expressly as Plutarch had wished, his writings then became a popular core for school curriculums. Before the vernacular had been accepted as suitable for classroom training, Plutarch was studied and digested in Latin. But with the coming of translations into currency, the commentaries of the Greek writer became readily accessible even for readers of limited education.

To be explicit, Plutarch was first introduced to a wide, popular reading public in 1559 with Jacques Amyot's successful rendering of the *Parallel Lives* into French. So seminal was Amyot's enterprise that European literary craftsmen never again could claim a lack of exciting portrayals from antiquity. It comes as no surprise that Thomas North, later to be knighted by Elizabeth for his remarkable feats of translation, put the *Lives* into English only twenty years after Amyot. In fact, North based his English translation on Amyot's text, not on an original Greek or later Latin version. Plutarch's *Moralia* also soon was brought out in the vernacular of several European countries. Amyot completed a French edition in 1572, while the learned Philemon Holland did the English in 1603. By the end of the sixteenth century, Plutarch legitimately can be said to have become a ubiquitous teacher in the more civilized sectors of the world. The results are easily discerned, as we shall see.

I *Beneficiaries of Plutarch's Legacy*

Literally dozens of the world's most celebrated thinkers and writers owe debts to Plutarch. The most striking factor to note about the legatees is that each borrows from Plutarch what interests him most, both in matters of substance and form. As one of the earliest formal biographers of Western civilization, he established precedents for all those following him who would be writers of lives.[2] Even though the art of biographical writing fell from prominence after the heights it had enjoyed during the Renaissance while purely historical studies ascended, there is no way to alter the fact that for fifteen hundred years Plutarch's biographical work was regarded as a fundamentally sound rendition of history.[3] One can also suggest that to assemble lives according to a common axis of belief, action, or role remains a valid entry into history today, as witness the great popularity of the late President John F. Kennedy's book *Profiles in Courage.* At the same time, Plutarch's *Moralia* established him as one of the world's first essayists. In this connection Douglas Bush writes: "While Plato and Cicero and Horace have contributed to the spirit and sometimes to the form of the modern essay, the classical prototypes are the moral works of Seneca and Plutarch." [4] Unlike the concept of parallel lives, the form of the essay gained ready support since Plutarch's lifetime; only a very few shapers of thought in history have avoided the essay as their vehicle of expression.[5] As for the content of Plutarch's endeavors, each subsequent reader tapped the facet of his thought that he required. From the countless references to Plutarch found throughout the ages, we can conclude that he is considered a philosopher and sage who spoke on behalf of a distant, idealized classical heritage. As such, he was for centuries Europe's schoolmaster.

II *Rulers of State Indebted to Plutarch*

In brief, Plutarch's influence was all-pervasive. Kings were to find comfort in his repeated insistence on obeisance within a societal scheme. Little wonder that a monarch like Henry IV of France should write his wife Maria de Medicis enthusiastic letters regarding Plutarch. In one such letter he wrote: "Plutarch always delights me with a fresh novelty. To love him is to love me; for he has been long time the instructor of my youth . . . . [Plutarch's writing] has been like my conscience, and has whispered in my ear many good suggestions and maxims for my conduct, and the government of my affairs." [6] Politicians of nonmonarchical persuasions also have been drawn to Plutarch because of the spellbinding portraits of successful classical governmental experiments furnished in his narratives. Perhaps one of the most conspicuous illustrations of a governmental theorist pleading his debt to Plutarch is the eighteenth-century Frenchman de Montesquieu. Like other educated youths in France at the time, de Montesquieu was raised studying the attainments of antiquity. As a result, as one observer has noted, ". . . his mind . . . was impregnated with an admiration for the Sparta of Plutarch's *Lycurgus,* for ancient Athens and the Roman Republic." [7] Oliver Goldsmith, in his Preface to Plutarch's *Lives,* cites a statement by de Montesquieu which best sums up the Frenchman's homage to the Greek biographer: "What Histories can be found (says the Marquis *De Montesquieu*) that please and instruct like the Lives of *Plutarch?*

. . . I am of the same Opinion with that Author, who said, that if he was constrained to fling all the Books of the Antients into the Sea, PLUTARCH *should be the last drowned.*" [8]

III *Ethical Spokesmen Making Use of Plutarch*

Making substantial use of Plutarch's essay style, as well as his fundamental ethical bias, are multitudes of religious leaders, educators, and moralists. Some salient examples among church fathers of various faiths are Jeremy Taylor and Cotton Mather, while Erasmus admits to a much more profound degree of borrowing. Taylor's extremely popular *Holy Living and Dying* echoes the predominant chord struck during the mid-seventeenth century in England. Studding the pages of his collection of sermons, prayers, and guiding dissertations are allusions to ethical rationales offered ages earlier by Plutarch. Taylor cites Plutarch by name innumerable times, and in certain footnotes provides the precise Plutarchian source, usually some piece from the *Moralia.* Chapter II of *Holy Living and Dying,* called "Of Christian Justice," taps Plutarch's essays repeatedly, particularly in those sections commenting on obedience owed to superiors. The remarks of the pagan Plutarch, it seems, were wholly welcomed into the verbal arsenal of Christian apologists when straightforward issues of ethical order and priority were concerned. In a section entitled "Rules for Married Persons," Taylor openly borrowed extensively from Plutarch's *Advice to Bride and Groom* (*Moralia,* Loeb volume 2).[9] Opening the treatise on cultivating a happy married life, the Reverend Taylor paraphrased Plutarch in words that had become almost commonplace for seventeenth-century Englishmen: "Husbands must give to their wives love, maintenance, duty, and the sweetness of conversation; and wives must pay to them all they have or can, with the interest of obedience and reverence: and they must be complicated in affections and interest, that there be no distinction between them of mine and thine. . . . The husband must rule over the wife, as the soul does over the body . . ." (142–43). Taylor's own footnotes at this point offer conclusive proof that he was citing Plutarch's commentary to support his argument, a situation not at all out of the ordinary for men of the cloth in Taylor's day.[10]

Even in the emerging America of the late seventeenth century, Plutarch's ethical authority found a seedbed in the Puritan zeal of

Cotton Mather. After all, Plutarch's fundamental moralism would appeal to the mind of Mather, while Plutarch's status as a pagan would not need to cause trouble with the Puritan sense of history. The American scholar Kenneth B. Murdock succinctly examines the situation of the Puritans in colonial America this way: ". . . as ardent Protestants they had a special interest in historical scholarship. For centuries earnest Christians had held a philosophy of history. The world proceeded according to divine plan. Even the story of the ages before Christ could be interpreted as the record of how the way was prepared for him." [11] Cotton Mather went on record as believing Plutarch necessary reading for "a person of good sense," and he considered the Greek "incomparable" as a teacher.[12] Furthermore, we should recall that great Christian teachers as early as the fourth century found much of value in Plutarch. The classicist Moses Hadas has pointed out that John Chrysostom, Gregory of Nazianz, Gregory of Nyssa, and the great Basil, employed Plutarch in their own teachings.[13]

Erasmus, that extraordinary epitome of the Renaissance humanist, was a close reader of Plutarch. Within the *Colloquies* of Erasmus, fully a dozen topics reflect titles almost identical to those of essays comprising the *Moralia.* A few illustrations might clarify the point. *A Feast of Many Courses* from the *Colloquies* reveals that Erasmus was well aware not only of regional mores but of classical antecedents as well, because several of the injunctions here derived from *Quaestiones conviviales* (*Table-Talk*) in Plutarch's *Moralia.* Similarly, Erasmus' *Marriage* is found nearly verbatim in Plutarch's *Advice to Bride and Groom,* while *The Poetic Feast, The Fabulous Feast, Sympathy,* and *Courtship*—all from the *Colloquies*—drew extensively from the *Moralia.* Erasmus writes in *The Godly Feast* that "This codex contains some short works of Plutarch, the *Moralia,* selected and skillfully copied by someone expert in Greek writing. So much piety do I find in them that I think it marvelous such Christian-like notions could have come into a pagan mind."[14]

Nor was Erasmus unique in his weighty appropriations from Plutarch. While analyzing certain of the *Colloquies,* the authority Craig R. Thompson announces the debt to Plutarch of Erasmus' age generally. Speaking of the stories recounted in *The Sober Feast,* Thompson asserts that "They come from Plutarch's *Lives* and *Moralia,* but some were common property too. Erasmus was fond of Plutarch. . . . No Greek writer is sounder on moral topics. . . . The sixteenth century shared this opinion."[15] And still more conclusive is Thompson's verdict about Erasmus and his commentary called *The New Mother:*

> His pronouncements on the importance of a mother's nursing her own child follow fairly closely the time-honored precepts of the essay in Plutarch's *Moralia* on bringing up children, *De liberis educandis, 5.* . . . No Greek writer was esteemed more highly by the sixteenth century. Erasmus shared this estimation, and he had published translations of some of the *Moralia.* . . . The Plutarchan counsel on children became common literary property. . . . In Renaissance literature Plutarch's advice . . . is repeated as an obvious truth.[16]

Among secular thinkers of different eras, Plutarch is in evidence as well. Again in the Renaissance, Plutarch's astute common sense appealed to those who themselves sought to educate their peers to the good life. Sir Thomas Elyot in his *Book Named the Governor* (1531) and in *Of The Knowledge Which Maketh a Wise Man* constructs his didactic works with adages of a strong ethical nature in the Plutarchian idiom. Additionally, he had published translations from Plutarch and thus knew the Greek sage well. Sir Walter Raleigh was inspired in part by Plutarch to set down his *History of the World,* because of Plutarch's concept of history as epic story and because of the historical data he had provided later generations.[17]

Three additional essayists of the highest order reveal the stamp of Plutarch. The *Essays* of Sir Francis Bacon, for example, even when scanned hurriedly, reflects by the titles of its individual components a close kinship to the *Moralia.* Several of the pieces dwell directly on Plutarchian antecedents. In Essay XVII, called "Of Superstition," Bacon commences his remarks by quoting Plutarch on the identical topic:

> It were better to have no opinion of God at all, than such an opinion as is unworthy of him: for the one is unbelief, the other is contumely: and certainly superstition is the reproach of the Deity. Plutarch saith well to that purpose: *Surely* (saith he) *I had rather a great deal men should say there was no such man at all as Plutarch, than that they should say that there was one Plutarch that would eat his children as soon as they were born;* as the poets speak of Saturn.[18]

Essay XL, "Of Fortune," similarly is deeply suffused with the notions of Plutarch's discussion with the same title from the *Moralia.* Other of the essays mirroring discernible resemblances with Plutarch's thoughts are "Of Death" (II), "Of Envy" (IX), "Of Atheism" (XVI), "Of Friendship" (XXVII), "Of the True Greatness of Kingdoms and Estates" (XXIX), "Of Youth and Age" (XLII) and "Of Followers and Friends" (XLVIII).[19]

In similar fashion, Rousseau eagerly admitted Plutarch's influence on the development of his thought. With Rousseau, however, the imprint was less that of direct borrowing of axioms. Rather, his entire outlook on the nature of life and history was significantly shaped by the accounts of the past given by Plutarch. Just "as Plutarch's *Lives* built the heroic ideal of the Elizabethan age,"[20] they likewise encouraged Rousseau "to interpret ancient civilizations in terms of heroic personalities."[21] And once more like Bacon, Rousseau went on record as having relied on Plutarch. When his *Discours* won him his first fame, Rousseau later humbly admitted in the *Confessions,* the success of that early piece "set working in my heart that primal leaven of heroism and virtue that my father, my country and Plutarch had placed there in my childhood."[22]

Long before Rousseau another Frenchman who profoundly altered the course of world thought had discovered the endearing qualities of Plutarch's writing. Michel de Montaigne was read assiduously by Western intellectuals, as well as by the greatest literary masters in France, England, Germany, and Spain during his lifetime at the close of the sixteenth century. Like his colleagues among the learned humanists of his day, Montaigne turned to the literature of the past both for personal pleasure and for the knowledge and instruction therein afforded. In his earlier contemplations, Montaigne showed himself a partisan of stoical thought as promulgated in the works of Seneca and as he believed he saw it in Plutarch. Gradually, however, Montaigne abandoned Seneca's theories for those of Plutarch which he considered less dogmatic and more human and moderate.[23]

The French authority on Montaigne, Pierre Villey, suggests the obvious about his subject's reliance on Plutarch: Montaigne was strongly attracted to the ancient Greek writer because of his charm *and* his humane, moral approach to history. In Villey's words, "The superiority of Plutarch over all other historians, according to Montaigne, stems from his attaching history to souls rather than to facts. . . . History, in Plutarch, is history treated by a moralist."[24] The result, according to Villey's exhaustive accounting, is over four hundred unquestionable borrowings from Plutarch in the *Essays*. Beyond providing Montaigne with authoritative wisdom from antiquity, Plutarch had a more direct salutary effect on him as a man. Quite literally, Plutarch assisted Montaigne in better comprehending himself and his world. Again to cite Villey's words, "The foremost service that Plutarch rendered Montaigne is the habit to observe himself objectively and to observe others around him."[25]

Naturally, Montaigne's own writing furnishes the most telling illustrations of his borrowings from Plutarch; nor is he reluctant to reveal those debts. In his article entitled "How One Ought to Govern His Will," from the *Essays* (III. 10), Montaigne states: "As Plutarch saith, that such as by the vice of bashfulness are soft and tractable to grant whatsoever is demanded, are afterward as prone and facile to recant and break their word. In like manner, he that enters lightly into a quarrel is subject to leave it as lightly."[26] Very self-revealing, also, is Montaigne's explanation (III. 5, in *Essays*) of his association with the Greek moralist: "He is so universal and so ample that for all occasions and whatever extravagant subject you have undertaken, he works his way into your efforts and extends to you a helpful hand liberally provided with inexhaustible riches and embellishments. . . ."[27] Small wonder, in light of such grateful admissions, that Montaigne was pleased to be called by some "the Christian Plutarch."[28]

IV *The Debts of Literary Artists to Plutarch*

Comprising the single largest body of Plutarch's legatees are countless literary notables over the centuries. The effect of having Plutarch's works within arm's reach of the culturally eager intellectuals of Europe (and soon thereafter of America, too) was impressive, as our earlier remarks have perhaps indicated. But the influence of Plutarch's writing was all the more profound among the *literati,* in particular. The numbers of writers drawing on Plutarch in one manner or another are astonishing. In England such authors as Sidney, Spenser, Ben Jonson, Shakespeare, Dryden, Milton, Herrick, Chapman, Beaumont, Fletcher, Swift, Walter

Landor, Wordsworth, Browning, Mary Shelley, and H. G. Wells reveal debts to the Greek moralist and biographer. Meanwhile, in the United States, Emerson and Melville became the most renowned literary figures to capitalize on Plutarch's writings.[29] Of the German literary giants, Goethe and Schiller appropriated from Plutarch.[30] Nor is it stretching the case to declare that French drama of the late sixteenth and entire seventeenth centuries was beholden to him for innumerable themes and materials from ancient times. A cursory look at the popular French dramatists from 1550 to 1700, to illustrate, shows that over two dozen had written a total of over forty plays based on or derived from Plutarch's narrative accounts and essays.[31] Henry Carrington Lancaster thus is well supported by numbers when he writes of seventeenth-century French theater: "So far as direct influence was concerned, that of Greek historians, especially of Plutarch, was greater than that of all other Greek writers combined." [32]

Perhaps a consideration in some detail of two masters of letters from different ages and locales, Shakespeare and Emerson, can assist in our measurements of Plutarch's impact on the literature of the world. In the case of Ralph Waldo Emerson, the effects come closest to mirroring both Plutarch's thought and his writing formats. Indeed, Emerson is the image of his Greek guide in many respects: as a unique deist with a pervasive moralistic approach to life, as a popular speaker who spread his personalized ethical gospel by way of wide lecturing at home and overseas, and as a well-intentioned crusader seeking to encourage a more natural worship and religion. Emerson all his life unashamedly announced his reliance on Plutarch for support.[33] On more than one occasion, Emerson declared that he and his fellow intellectuals were "more indebted to him [i.e., to Plutarch] than to all the ancient writers." [34] Nor was his simply an infatuation with the congeniality of the Greek commentator. Emerson's life-long concern remained to improve man's tenure on earth, and he would not permit himself to be distracted by a honey-tongued mountebank, no matter how humane sounding. All the same, for him the finest achievement of Plutarch was his ability to remain intellectually effective while sustaining his own personal cordiality. In an analytic introduction to a collection of Plutarch's essays, Emerson wrote: ". . . what specially marks him, he is a chief example of the illumination of the intellect by the force of morals. Though the most amiable of boon-companions, this generous religion gives him *aperçus* like Goethe's." [35]

Students of Emerson must come to grips with his concept of "moral sentiment." But once it is comprehended that Emerson admired the ubiquitous moralizing of Plutarch and that he appropriated both much of the tone and substance from the writing of the Greek, we more easily can grasp Emerson's basic philosophical posture, one with a secularist slant. He wrote in his *Journals* that "God never cants. And the charm of Plutarch and Plato and Thucydides for me, I believe, is that there I get ethics without cant." [36] Plutarch's essay *Superstition*, we may recall, argues precisely against cant in religious theory. Further, the unpretentious view of friendship espoused by Emerson in his essay of that title belies its Plutarchian prototype in a similarly named work almost two thousand years earlier. Emerson's words are: "There are two elements that go to the composition of friendship, each so sovereign that I can detect no superiority in either, no reason why either should be first named. One is truth. . . . The other element of friendship is tenderness." [37]

In yet another key respect Emerson followed a path long before blazed by Plutarch, the writing of biographies. His *Journal* entry dated 1832 announces his ambitions: "The British Plutarch and the modern Plutarch is yet to be written. . . . I would draw characters, not write lives. I would evoke the spirit of each, and their relics might rot." [38] What attracted Emerson so forcefully to Plutarch's biographical method was the heroic grandeur which spoke from beneath every life. Within the heroic conduct depicted by the Greek mentor lay the ethical model for all subsequent generations. In his essay "Heroism," Emerson explains, "But if we explore the literature of Heroism, we shall quickly come to Plutarch, who is its Doctor and historian." [39] Plutarch's most striking figures from the *Parallel Lives* exhibited to a remarkable degree the very characteristics held at a premium by both Plutarch and Emerson: endurance in the face of suffering, pursuit of a moral path to goodness, and a recognition of the temporal quality of human existence.

The world, thought Emerson, needed heroes exemplifying proper behavior to emulate, not rigid injunctions from inflexible religious apologists. In another entry in his *Journals*, Emerson wrote disparagingly of a speech he had just heard, the antidote for which he proposed a dose of Plutarch: "Yesterday Mr. Mann's Address on Education. It was full of the modern gloomy view of our democratical institutions, and hence the inference to the importance of schools. . . . A Life in Plutarch would be a perfect rebuke to such a sad discourse. If Christianity is effete, let us try the doctrine of power to endure."[40] Plutarch's accounts of impressive human performance in his subjects were befitting to Emerson's own time, he asserted, because in his view of history Emerson saw no particular improvement in human nature. As he commented in his essay "The Individual," there were no greater men in his own time "than Plutarch's heroes who flourished three or four and twenty centuries ago."[41] When he undertook to offer biographies for figures of a more modern era, then, Emerson could continue to employ the same measuring sticks as did Plutarch in assessing a particular man's accomplishments in life. Although Emerson's biographies and lectures on famous personages cannot bear a point by point comparison with Plutarch's, yet he did utilize several of the techniques of Plutarch in comments on Michelangelo, Burke, Luther, George Washington, Milton, Carlyle, Thoreau, and Lincoln.

Finally, even if men of the modern ages could not reveal themselves as superior to the ancients in Emerson's theory, they could be as sound, at least. Emerson's words are high praise from one learned in the past. For Emerson, that fact established a kinship of all men, of all ages, whereby the affinities between men's deeds always could be seen despite chronological and spatial separations. Thus Emerson exclaims concerning Montaigne's relationship with Plutarch: "It is one of the felicities of literary history, the tie which inseparably couples these two names across fourteen centuries" to comprise the "best example of the universal citizenship and fraternity of the human mind."[42]

Most celebrated of all Plutarch's beneficiaries is Shakespeare. What the Bard retained from Plutarch is uniquely his own, when compared to the borrowings of more didactic essayists such as Montaigne, Erasmus, or Emerson. As we have observed, those writers worked their way through Plutarch's extensive writings, relishing the ethical pronouncements therein to be tasted. For them, Plutarch served as a mirror of past cultures and as evidence of the continuum of human nature. Plutarch's concerns with behavior and the human condition were matched by those of subsequent intellectuals like Montaigne and Emerson. With Shakespeare, too, there is a duality of carryovers from Plutarch with respect to both substance and writing pattern, except that the Elizabethan playwright cast his interest in character into a dramatic mold for the stage. Since the name of Shakespeare is the best known among authors in the Western world, it is to be expected that Shakespeare be regarded as Plutarch's most spectacular pupil.

As with others before him and since, Shakespeare's attraction to Plutarch commenced when he had a copy of Plutarch's books before him in translation. Once he had delved into the *Lives*, Shakespeare became a confirmed student of Plutarch, as scholars like T. J. B. Spencer, C. F. Tucker Brooke, and Walter Skeat conclusively have established.[43] On the basis of his plays, nonetheless, it is seen that, though Shakespeare read Plutarch in part to evoke the ethos of the Greco-Roman past, his principal concern remained anchored in Plutarch's projection of character in conflict. Shakespeare's drama, it will be recalled, was produced in his day without any wholehearted attempt to reproduce the ancient Roman or Greek background in a realistic style. Production techniques and stage props and settings in Elizabethan drama were not geared for any such detailed re-creation of costume drama from another era; and actors' garb remained essentially simplified versions of Elizabethan clothing with stylized touches added by way of capes, stage swords, and helmets to aid the dramatic illusion. Rather, as with nearly all Plutarch's readers, Shakespeare felt the drawing force of the heroic personages and deeds of Plutarch's accounts, those grand figures bigger than ordinary men, in conflict with the world and their position in it.

Caius Marcius Coriolanus, to illustrate, was depicted by Plutarch as a superb Roman warrior who never flinched in the face of battle and seemingly certain destruction. At the same time, Plutarch recounted events that revealed the inflexible distaste Coriolanus possessed for the Roman commoners. Eventually, after Rome ungratefully had exiled Coriolanus by way of underhanded means, Coriolanus allied himself with enemies of Rome and prepared to destroy her. While he was camped outside the city gates awaiting the next morning when the final blow would be administered to Rome, his mother Volumnia, as a last resort, went to Coriolanus to entreat for mercy for Rome. After an exhaustive appeal, she did manage to change his mind, amazingly enough. Plutarch relates the crucial moment this way:

> And with these words she threw herself at his feet, together with his wife and children. Then Marcius, crying out "What hast thou done to me, my mother!" lifted her up, and pressing her right hand warmly, said: "Thou art victorious, and thy victory means good fortune to my country, but death to me; for I shall withdraw vanquished, though by thee alone." (LCL, *Life of Caius Marcius Coriolanus,* IV. 36. 209)

Shakespeare renders the historic event in strikingly similar words in his play *Coriolanus,* indicating that this master of language found little need for additional embellishments or elaborations:

> O mother, mother!
> What have you done? Behold, the heavens do ope,
> The gods look down, and this unnatural scene
> They laugh at. O my mother, mother! O!
> You have won a happy victory to Rome;
> But for your son—believe it, O believe it!—
> Most dangerously you have with him prevailed,
> If not most mortal to him. But let it come.
> (V. iii. 182–89; *Coriolanus,* ed. Harry Levin, *The Pelican Shakespeare* [Baltimore, 1965])

Nor was Shakespeare forced to create his own credible psychological motivation for the capitulation of the stern soldier to the pleas of a woman, even when it meant abandoning his plan for personal revenge on a city which had insulted him beyond limit. Plutarch early in the *Life* involved had laid the necessary groundwork. There, he commented on Coriolanus' excessive partiality for his widowed mother who had been left to raise him alone: "Marcius, who thought he owed his mother the filial gratitude also which would have been due to his father, could not get his fill of gladdening and honouring Volumnia, nay, he even married according to her wish and request, and continued to live in the same house with his mother after children were born to him" (LCL, IV. 4. 127). The filial attachment, stronger even than the thirst for vengeance, was thus ready at hand when Shakespeare began adapting the antique tale into one of the most brooding and provocative tragedies of all time. Coriolanus' very life, as transmitted through Plutarch, furnished the needed tragic flaw which was to take the protagonist to his doom.

Equally appealing to Shakespeare's sense of true drama in life were Plutarch's colorful descriptions of influential persons out of the past. Consequently, when he fastened upon the Cleopatra portrayed in Plutarch for a play of love and intrigue, Shakespeare only did what other dramatists had done before him (as the Frenchmen Jodelle and Garnier and the Englishman Daniel) and after (as Dryden and Shaw). Plutarch describes the first meeting of Antony and Cleopatra with full, effective details, making it simple to comprehend the powerful charisma of the famed "Serpent of the Nile":

> . . . she came sailing up the river Cydnus, in a barge with gilded stern and outspread sails of purple, while oars of silver beat time to the music of flutes and fifes and harps. She herself lay all along under a canopy of cloth of gold, dressed as Venus in a picture, and beautiful young boys, like painted Cupids, stood on each side to fan her. Her maids were dressed like sea nymphs and graces, some steering at the rudder, some working at the ropes. The perfumes diffused themselves from the vessel to the shore, which was covered with multitudes, part following the galley up the river on either bank, part running out of the city to see the sight. The market-place was quite emptied, and Antony was left alone sitting upon the tribunal. . . .[44]

The exotic qualities of Cleopatra's entry into Antony's life were not lost on Shakespeare. With very few alterations of the rich descriptions offered by Plutarch, the playwright in his *Antony and Cleopatra* deftly recast the account into lines of poetry now burned into the memory of each succeeding generation of readers and playgoers. It is Shakespeare's Enobarbus who immortalizes the fateful incident in the play:

> The barge she sat in, like a burnished throne
> Burned on the water: the poop was beaten gold;
> Purple the sails, and so perfumed that
> The winds were love-sick with them; the oars were silver,
> Which to the tune of flutes kept stroke, and made
> The water which they beat to follow faster,
> As amorous of their strokes. For her own person,

It beggared all description: she did lie
In her pavilion, cloth-of-gold, of tissue,
O'er-picturing that Venus where we see
The fancy outwork nature. On each side her
Stood pretty dimpled boys, like smiling Cupids,
With divers-colored fans. . . .
. . . .
From the barge
A strange invisible perfume hits the sense
Of the adjacent wharfs. The city cast
Her people out upon her; and Antony,
Enthroned i'the market-place, did sit alone,
Whistling to the air; which, but for vacancy,
Had gone to gaze on Cleopatra too,
And made a gap in nature.
(II. ii. 191–203, 211–18; *Antony and Cleopatra*, ed. C. J. Gianakaris, Blackfriars Shakespeare [Dubuque, 1969])

Because of passages such as those cited here, which display Shakespeare's close verse approximation to Plutarch's sources, the celebrated Shakespearean authority C. F. Tucker Brooke was led to declare that "Nowhere else in Shakespeare is there an instance of verbal borrowing at the height of dramatic intensity which is comparable to these."[45] In addition to *Antony and Cleopatra* and *Coriolanus*, Shakespeare was inspired in his *Julius Caesar* by Plutarch's *Life of Julius Caesar* and *Life of Marcus Brutus*. *Timon of Athens* owed much of its central plot line to a digression in Plutarch's *Life of Marcus Antonius*, while *The Life of Theseus* furnished touches to Shakespeare's comedy *A Midsummer Night's Dream*. Beyond these indubitable borrowings from Plutarch, one can only conjecture about further loans. Shakespeare no doubt read additional *Lives* with interest, and scholars point to those of *Alcibiades*, *Pompeius*, *Cicero*, and *Cato, the Younger* as most likely perused by the Bard; yet we can offer no conclusive proof. Nor can we pursue such possibilities any further here. Modern readers can content themselves with the available exhaustive explorations into this matter by Brooke, Skeat, and Spencer, as already indicated. Suffice it to say that several of Shakespeare's finest tragedies directly draw both plot contours and character juices from Plutarch to an extent unparalleled in any other of his borrowings.

Without question, Plutarch had an effect on Shakespeare in many more general, nonliterary ways, as well. The stately quasi-Stoicism in Plutarch which impressed other Renaissance thinkers like Bacon and Montaigne similarly helped inform Shakespeare's cosmic view, particularly with respect to the inevitability of destiny. Further, Shakespeare's knowledge of near contemporaries like Montaigne meant that he was open in an indirect fashion to Plutarch through them as intermediaries. The stories told by the Greek and his wide-ranging moral essays were ubiquitous in all of Europe during Shakespeare's lifetime. It would have been extraordinary, therefore, had he not amassed a considerable debt to Plutarch.

V *A Final Assessment of Plutarch and His Achievements*

Our explorations of the man and his times lead us to one certain conclusion; namely, that Plutarch constitutes a fascinating phenomenon in several respects. In a very pragmatic sense, he proved invaluable for the variety and amount of knowledge from classical times which he conveyed to the modern world. In this study we have aspired to suggest the range of information he passed on directly to his literary heirs. To test just how essential that data has been, imagine Erasmus or Emerson stating their cases without Plutarch's supportive discussions, or Shakespeare seeking to pen his Roman tragedies without Plutarch's singular models of key Roman characters. If this final chapter has succeeded, readers can begin to sense the hypothetical destitution of thought and literary art had Plutarch *not* lived or had his works *not* been perpetuated.

At the same time, readers today recognize that other commentators from antiquity also furnished historical accounts. What is not transmitted in their works, however, is the unique temperament possessed by Plutarch. As we have surveyed them here, writers from different eras have been attracted to the humanistic spell Plutarch evoked. While recounting the events and deeds comprising the lives of his heroes, he could retain the minimum detachment required for objective narrative. But when an ethical scruple played too large a role in the conduct of a character he was describing, Plutarch relentlessly would make the fault known. Thus he projected a didactic moralism within an air of sweet logic. Within a cosmic view that was conventional for his day,

Plutarch acknowledged the enormous part played by chance in the external circumstances of one's existence. By way of that tacit admission, Plutarch without knowing it reflected a stoical facet in his thought, despite his open disavowal of that system. Later readers of Plutarch discerned the hard-headed quality in his writing which rejected as false the sanguine view that men could or would act properly in every situation. As a result, even his grandest hero Alexander behaved inexcusably on occasion, and the brilliant Cicero restricted the success of his career by a prattling that lacked discretion. Men were not perfect, in Plutarch's eyes, an acknowledged fact which prohibited him from viewing life behind rose-colored glasses.

Counterpoised with Plutarch's recessive stoicism stands the more central component in his world view, humanism. According to the humanistic premise, though man is not perfect, he certainly possesses the capacities at least to strive for perfectibility. The dozen or so years he devoted to administrative functions at Delphi irrevocably reinforced for Plutarch the humanistic faith in self-knowledge and self-discipline. The carved slogans in the Delphic temple, "Know Thyself" and "Avoid Extremes," were always in sight to remind Plutarch of the essential codes for living the good life. Additionally, underlying these tenets stood a positive, even optimistic, base: accept the personal responsibility of each of us to examine life constantly, and then master one's self accordingly. By way of the self-determination thereby effected, man had an opportunity to shape his destiny insofar as that was possible. At that juncture Plutarch was poised between the pessimism of stoicism and the optimism of humanism. The randomness of fortune partially was counterbalanced by purposeful actions that resulted when a person held control of his conduct. In Plutarch's uneasy formula, responsibility was juxtaposed with chance. Mark Antony, as a result, was author of his own downfall in Plutarch's estimate. The recipient of extraordinary admiration and loyalty from his soldiers, Antony thoughtlessly squandered his reasoning nature to idle away precious time with the Egyptian siren Cleopatra. Plutarch's assessment of the circumstances, if not outright disdainful of Antony, remains blunt. Demetrius, with whom Antony is matched in the *Lives,* was guilty of many similar flaws in character. Still, even he comes off better than Antony in a comparison. Plutarch judges them this way:

Both were insolent in prosperity, and abandoned themselves to luxuries and enjoyments. Yet it cannot be said that Demetrius, in his revellings and dissipations, ever let slip the time for action; pleasures with him attended only the superabundance of his ease . . . . he never incurred disaster through indolence or self-indulgence. Whereas Antony . . . was over and over again disarmed by Cleopatra, and beguiled away, while great actions and enterprises of the first necessity fell, as it were, from his hands, to go with her to the seashore of Canopus and Taphosiris, and play about. And in the end, like another Paris, he left the battle to fly to her arms. . . . Antony fled first, and, following Cleopatra, abandoned his victory. . . . For their final disasters they have both only to thank themselves. . . .[46]

Character does indeed have a vital bearing on fate for Plutarch. He consequently remains unimpressed by the renowned Antony whose faulted character led to a disappointing end. The key term in Plutarch's discussion is Antony's "self-indulgence," a trait anathema to the dedicated humanist for whom responsibility was the correct keynote. Nor, we may recall, was Alexander's premature death attributable to any particular design of the gods. Instead, the fever resulting from a mundane drinking bout brought low the most illustrious Greek leader of classical history.

Because men could substantively influence their own careers despite an ever-present stoical shadow in life, Plutarch emphasized the humanistic potentialities of mankind in all he wrote. Similarly, he led his own life according to the same guidelines he advocated for others. Plutarch's celebrated letter solacing his grieving wife over the loss of their daughter, by its tone and advice, could have been addressed to any mourning parent. He responded to a personal tragedy just as he would have to that of someone unknown. He never contented himself with abstaining from the daily bruises of life. A humanistic activist to the last, he returned to Chaeronea from an extended triumphant lecture tour in Rome in order to meet the challenges faced by a poor village in conquered Greece, far from the hub of Roman activity. Nor did he turn away from the fading fortunes of Delphi. Instead, he devoted his attention to the plight of the Delphic temple in particular and to that ailment of the expiring Greek religion in general. Thanks to the many years he spent at Delphi, nursing the religious establishment there, the Delphic Oracle enjoyed a brief revival for a while. Plutarch welcomed worthy challenges, basing his personal life as well as his intellectualized doctrines on the humanist's premise that reason when properly applied makes positive things happen. It is Plutarch's dedication to service on behalf of his fellows that also permeates his life's actions and writings. That unflagging devotion to a mankind equally vulnerable and filled with potential for good thrusts Plutarch far above typical correspondents from the past.

As a consequence, readers always have responded to the warmth and humanity of Plutarch the man, as well as to Plutarch the historian-moralist. Thomas North, in the dedication "To the Reader" which heads his English translation of the *Lives,* mirrors the representative reaction of all ages to Plutarch's magnetism:

> Nowe for the Author, I will not denye but love may deceive me, for I must needes love him with whome I have taken so much payne: but I beleve I might be bold to affirme, that he hath written the profitablest story of all Authors. . . . But this man being excellent in wit, learning, and experience, hath chosen the speciall actes of the best persons, of the famosest nations of the world.[47]

Plutarch intrigues readers on another general count as a specimen component within the historical phenomenon called the Renaissance. The value of Plutarch to his own day is beyond dispute. As our opening chapter brought to light, honors of all kinds were awarded him during his lifetime: honorary Roman citizenship for his lectures, civil governorships for his political ability, and monuments dedicated to him for uninterrupted, devoted service to mankind universally. Yet Plutarch, like so many writer-philosophers during the classical eras, easily might have vanished for good during the black days of barbarism which succeeded Roman domination of the Western world. Even as it stands now, classicists estimate that the large body of Plutarch's writing represents perhaps not much more than one-third of his work once extant.[48] Our fate in the modern age, then, might have been the same experienced with other great literary masters of antiquity like Menander, whom Plutarch admired enthusiastically (see, for instance, his *The Summary of a Comparison Between Aristophanes and Menander* from *Moralia,* LCL, volume X). Bits and pieces of writing by such celebrated authors still are being rediscovered to add fragments to the puzzle, piece by piece. Meanwhile, for those only partially recovered from the past, over-all evaluations remain impossible because the larger picture of their achievements is incomplete.[49]

The chance element in Plutarch's instance, we should admit, was kind to him. His writings, varied in subject as they were, assured them sufficient interest among strategic intellectuals during the largely nonliterate Middle Ages, with the result that many pieces were kept from oblivion. When the myriad of requisite conditions meshed together around the tenth century and what we generally call the Renaissance came into being, Plutarch's commentaries were able to surface again. Even then, on the other hand, their position at the forefront of the culture of the Renaissance was not firmly established in their then Latin version. Our observations earlier in the chapter suggest that one further step had to be mounted before the transmission of Plutarch's reservoir from antiquity could be accomplished for the modern eras: translations of the pieces into new vernacular languages in which populaces at large could enjoy access to the concepts and narratives.

For a wide reading audience, the light of Plutarch's knowledge was switched on first in France in 1559 with Amyot's provocative translation of the *Lives* into French. Soon thereafter, Germany and England followed suit with versions both of the *Parallel Lives* and the *Moralia* in their respective tongues. Through these editions, which in large measure were sparked by the whole impetus of the Renaissance spirit toward a revival of the classics from the past, Plutarch's fame was assured once and for all. Popular from the beginning in the borrowed languages of Western lands, Plutarch's work swiftly spread into the intellectual, literate fiber of the host peoples. The concrete results of Plutarch's massive influence in Europe and later America have only been touched in this chapter. Even so, it should be obvious that the thoughts and histories of Plutarch have become ubiquitous, turning up in direct or modified forms in almost all learned authors since the blooming of the Renaissance—and in some instances even before, as among church fathers.

In light of these factors, one final question may disturb the reader of today: If Plutarch formerly possessed such significance with respect to history, philosophy, religion, and biography, why is he not still in the foreground? No single answer is possible, though some scholars have given thought to the matter.[50] Several plausible diagnoses are possible. Like his Roman counterparts in letters, such as Cicero, Quintilian, and Horace, Plutarch enjoyed his very widest reading audience when the popular appeal of his works in the vernacular was reinforced or supplemented by the emphasis lent them through classically oriented academic curricula. Until the middle 1800s, a finer education in the West, for example, meant a thorough grounding in Greek and Latin, both in the languages and the literatures. With the spectacular widening of opportunities in education beginning during the last half of the nineteenth century came a pronounced shift toward modern cultures and tongues. Without continued direct exposure to the young, the full weight of Plutarch's knowledge was to be lost on the masses, even if not among scholars.

At the same time, by our present age most of Plutarch's stimulating commentaries have been assimilated into more recent philosophical and literary frameworks, such as those noted here by Montaigne, Shakespeare, Jonson, Milton, Goethe, Rousseau, Swift, Wordsworth, Emerson, and the rest. In a very legitimate sense, Plutarch's works have been transmuted, brought into modern currency, just as he had salvaged writers before him who might otherwise have become extinct. It is not valid, consequently, to think of Plutarch as "dead," as we think of classical languages like Greek and Latin. Rather, in direct and indirect fashions, his work has been redistributed through subsequent literary artists and philosophers. His thoughts consequently remain very much alive and operative today.

Nor, indeed, has his writing itself lost its appeal for readers now. Narratives and essays of Plutarch are to found in innumerable books today, while, more importantly, perhaps, selections from Plutarch are readily available to average nonacademic readers as well through several paperback editions. Everywhere one turns, in fact, one comes face to face with nuggets of information from the Greek Sage, such as the charm of Cleopatra, the correct conduct of an auditor at a lecture, the gentlemanliness of Brutus, the control of one's passions through self-knowledge, and so on. The evidence of his continued viability surrounds us now as it always has, even if partly disguised within more modern formats employed by recent authors.

We are fortunate in another matter of chance concerning Plutarch. He lived to an advanced age and thus was permitted to set down his ideas with amplitude, both the profound concepts and the quotidian chatter. But even had he died at a far younger age, his name would have been established among the great of antiquity. As he wrote: "The measure of life is its excellence, not its length in years." Of the excellence of his life there is no doubt, for he brought together intellectual curiosity regarding the cosmos, scholarly research into the past, and an unfailing devotion to the life of the present, emblemized in a lifetime of service to his fellow men.

Notes and References

Chapter One

1. Quoted in R. H. Barrow, *Plutarch And His Times* (London, 1967), p. 71.
2. J. A. K. Thomson, *The Classical Background of English Literature* (New York, 1962), p. 107. Also, consider Moses Hadas, *Ancilla To Classical Reading* (Morningside Heights, N. Y., 1962), p. 310.
3. "In the last two centuries B. C. there was a heavy drain on the accumulated wealth of Greece, her regular income being insufficient to cover the cost of wars." See: Rostovtzeff, II, 1145.
4. Rostovtzeff, II, 1312.
5. J. and W. Langhorne, "Introduction," *Plutarch's Lives,* trans. John Dryden, rev. by A. H. Clough (New York, n.d.), p. xvi.
6. "Introduction" to *Plutarch's Lives,* Vol. I, trans. Bernadotte Perrin, Loeb Classical Library (Cambridge, Mass., and London, 1959), p. xi.
7. Julian Hibbert, "A Life of Plutarchus," *Plutarchus, And Theophrastus, On Superstition* (Kentish Town, England, 1828), p. 14.
8. J. and W. Langhorne, "Introduction," p. xvi.
9. Barrow, p. 36.
10. See the anonymous "Romios and Hellene," *TLS,* No. 3358 (July 7, 1966), 586.
11. Stringfellow Barr, *The Mask of Jove: A History of Graeco-Roman Civilization from the Death of Alexander to the Death of Constantine* (Philadelphia and New York, 1966), p. 307.
12. Barr, p. 311.
13. Edith Hamilton, *The Echo of Greece* (New York, 1957), p. 184.
14. Barr, pp. 328–29.
15. "He also resorted to legislative action to check the unpuritanical tendencies of his age. The Julian Laws of 19 and 18 B.C. aimed at the restoration of family life, the encouragement of marriage. . . . By example as well as by precept, Augustus sought to check the luxurious tendencies of the age. . . ." See: Arthur E. R. Boak and William G. Sinnigen, *A History of Rome to A. D. 565,* 5th ed. (New York, 1965), p. 281.

16. Barr, p. 311.
17. Gilbert Murray, *A History of Ancient Greek Literature* (London, 1907), p. 393.
18. Boak and Sinnigen, pp. 306–29.
19. Boak and Sinnigen, p. 390.
20. Barrow does not hesitate to claim of Plutarch that "by the time of his second visit to Rome his fame was considerable" (p. 39).
21. Barrow, p. 43.
22. Richard C. Trench, *Plutarch: His Life, His Lives and His Morals* (London, 1873), p. 8.
23. See Chapter 6 of Barrow's book for a fuller discussion.
24. Barrow, p. 42.
25. H. W. Parke and D. E. W. Wormell, *The Delphic Oracle,* Vol. I (Oxford, 1956), 277–79.
26. Parke and Lormell, I, 283.
27. Werner Jaeger, *Paideia: The Ideals of Greek Culture,* 2nd ed., trans. Gilbert Highet, Vol. I (New York, 1960), 300.
28. Parke and Wormell, I, 284–85.
29. Parke and Wormell furnish the intriguing final declarations attributed to the expiring oracle at Delphi: "Tell the king, the fairwought hall has fallen to the ground. No longer has Phoebus a hut, nor a prophetic laurel, nor a spring that speaks. The water of speech even is quenched." See: Vol. I, 20.
30. See the "Inscription Found at Delphi," titled photograph facing the title page of Volume I of *Plutarch's Moralia,* trans. Frank Cole Babbitt, in the Loeb Classical Library (Cambridge, Mass., and London, 1956).
31. Students of ethics from the Far East may be astonished at the resemblance here between Plutarch's axioms and those of Confucius.

Chapter Two

1. *A History of Ancient Greek Literature* (London, 1907), p. 396.
2. M. I. Finley, in a review of R. H. Barrow's *Plutarch and His Times* (Bloomington, Indiana, 1967), in the *New York Review of Books* (September 14, 1967), Vol. IX, no. 4, 29–30. Hereafter cited as Finley.
3. J. P. Mahaffy, *The Greek World Under Roman Sway: From Polybius to Plutarch* (London and New York, 1890), pp. 291–92.
4. Bernadotte Perrin, "Preface," *Plutarch's Themistocles and Aristides* (New York and London, 1901), p. ix. Hereafter cited as Perrin, *Themistocles.*
5. "Consider how uneasily biography lies between historical writing and belles lettres, somewhat disdainfully claimed by both." Given in:

Paul Murray Kendall, *The Art of Biography* (New York, 1965), p. 3. Hereafter cited as Kendall.

6. Oliver Goldsmith, "Preface," *Plutarch's Lives,* in the *Collected Works of Oliver Goldsmith,* ed. Arthur Friedman, Vol. V (Oxford, 1966), 226.

7. Kendall, p. 4.

8. The historian Finley is quite right in concluding that ". . . it is self-defeating to approach Plutarch from modern conventions of historical biography. He worked in a totally different tradition" (p. 30).

9. J. A. K. Thomson, *The Classical Background of English Literature* (New York, 1962), p. 106. Professor Kendall (p. 31) offers 1000 B.C. as marking the commencement of biographies and autobiographies, but he provides no details or authorities for his date.

10. H. L. Tracy, "Notes on Plutarch's Biographical Method," *The Classical Journal,* Vol. XXXVII (1941–42), 214–15. Also, see: Sir Richard C. Jebb, "Literature," Chapter III, in *A Companion to Greek Studies,* 3rd ed., ed. Leonard Whibley (Cambridge, 1916), p. 182.

11. R. H. Barrow, *Plutarch and His Times* (London, 1967), pp. 156–60. Among Latin historians referred to by Plutarch are Varro, Cato, Cicero, Livy, Caesar, Sallust, Augustus, as well as two dozen others, according to Barrow (p. 151).

12. *Plutarch* [:] *His Life, His Lives and His Morals* (London, 1873). Hereafter given as Trench.

13. Trench, p. 31.

14. Trench, p. 32.

15. Perrin, *Themistocles,* p. 5.

16. Perrin, *Themistocles,* pp. 9–10.

17. Stringfellow Barr, *The Mask of Jove* (Philadelphia and New York, 1966), p. 348. Also, consult: Moses Hadas, trans., "Introduction" to Plutarch's *On Love, The Family, and the Good Life*: *Selected Essays of Plutarch* (New York, 1957), p. 8.

18. Robert Flacelière, *A Literary History of Greece,* trans. Douglas Garman (Chicago, 1964), p. 359.

19. An astute observer like Oliver Goldsmith in his "Preface" to *Plutarch's Lives,* Vol. V, for example, lucidly enunciated the process: "An ingenious gentleman of my acquaintance, when asked what was the best lesson for youth? answered, *The life of a good man*: being asked, what was the next best? replied, *The life of a bad one*; for that the first would make him in love with virtue, and teach him how to conduct himself through life, so as to become an ornament to society, and a blessing to his family and friends; and the last would point out the hateful and horrid consequences of vice, and make him careful to avoid those actions which appeared so detestable in others" (227).

20. See: C. Kerenyi, *The Heroes of the Greeks* (New York, 1960).

21. Strange to say, the Loeb edition shows May as the founding month in the Greek text (p. 120), while the English translation of the same passage gives April. The discrepancy is nowhere reconciled in the volume.

Chapter Three

1. Normally in the writings of the ancient Greeks, the term "barbarian" (with or without a capital "B") means foreigner or non-Hellene. The Trojan, Persian, Egyptian, Lydian, and Taurian always were considered "barbarian," as were people from Cyprus, Crete, and Lemnos. But persons from bordering states such as Macedon sometimes were considered Hellenes, sometimes barbarian. In the account of Alexander here, it appears that Plutarch considers the Macedonians part of the larger Hellenic circle, at least for that moment in history. Some clarification on this point is available in: Helen H. Bacon, *Barbarians in Greek Tragedy* (New Haven, 1961).

2. Richard C. Trench, *Plutarch* [:] *His Life, His Lives and His Morals* (London, 1873), p. 73.

3. Leon Edel, "A Proud Papa Speaks Up," *Book Week* (March 21, 1965), 2.

Chapter Four

1. F. A. Wright, *A History of Later Greek Literature* (New York, 1932), p. 212.

2. Gilbert Highet, *The Classical Tradition* (New York, 1966), p. 119. For a negative opinion of the essays, see: J. P. Mahaffy, *The Greek World Under Roman Sway* (London and New York, 1890), p. 321.

3. Richard C. Trench, *Plutarch* [:] *His Life, His Lives and His Morals* (London, 1873), p. 73.

4. Frank Cole Babbitt, "Introduction," *Plutarch's Moralia,* Vol. III, trans. Frank Cole Babbitt (Cambridge, Mass. and London, 1949), 4. Another observer believes that the materials are based on conversations for the most part: see J. and W. Langhorne, "Introduction," *Plutarch's Lives,* Dryden's translation, revised by A. H. Clough (New York, n. d.), p. xviii.

5. R. H. Barrow, *Plutarch and His Times* (London, 1967), p. 42.

6. *Plutarch's Moralia,* Vol. II, trans. Frank C. Babbitt (Cambridge, Mass., and London, 1956). Because the Loeb volumes alone will be cited, all references to the *Moralia* will provide first the volume number from the Loeb series, then the sectional numeral within the essay, and last the page number. Three remaining volumes of the Loeb *Moralia,* VIII, XIII, and XV, have yet to be published. Only when

they are completed will there be a reliable English translation available of the entire *Moralia.*

7. *Plutarch's Moralia,* Vol. X, trans. Harold North Fowler (1960).

8. Edmund G. Berry, *Emerson's Plutarch* (Cambridge, Mass., 1961), p. 4.

9. *Plutarch's Moralia,* Vol. VII (1959), as translated by Phillip H. DeLacy and Benedict Einarson.

10. Plato's wise men include Myson instead of Anacharsis whom Plutarch inserts. For fuller information, see the "Introduction" to the dialogue in Volume II.

11. *Plutarch's Moralia,* trans. Frank C. Babbitt (1960).

12. An interesting execution of several performer/auditor relationships is found in Thomas Mann's brilliant short story called "The Infant Prodigy."

13. Plutarch here and elsewhere places much credence in the notion that the father's condition at the moment of conceiving his offspring affects the child. Hence a father who is drunk when begetting progeny probably passes drunkenness on to the child (I. 3. 7), while a man in a gay mood when procreating might well produce a child cheery in disposition (*On The Delays of the Divine Vengeance,* Loeb VII. 20. 263).

14. Berry, *Emerson's Plutarch,* p. 16. Also see Charles Read Baskervill's "Introduction," *Plutarch's Quyete of Mynde,* trans. Thomas Wyat (reproduced in facsimile from the copy in the Henry E. Huntington Library).

15. Frederick Morgan Padelford, ed. and trans., *Essays on the Study and Use of Poetry by Plutarch and Basil the Great,* Yale Studies in English, Vol. XV (New York, 1902), p. 13.

16. Frank C. Babbitt, "Introduction," Vol. IV of Loeb *Moralia,* trans. by Frank C. Babbitt (1957), 3–5.

17. *Plutarch's Moralia,* Vol. V, trans. Frank C. Babbitt (1962).

18. The dialogue is found in Vol. XII of the Loeb *Moralia,* trans. Harold Cherniss and William C. Helmbold (1957).

19. It should be noted that both volumes XIII and XIV in the Loeb translations concentrate largely on pro-Platonic and anti-Epicurean essays.

20. A thorough consideration of Plutarch's daemonic theories is available in Guy Soury's *La Démonologie de Plutarque* (Paris, 1942).

21. George Depue Hadzsits, *Prolegomena to a Study of the Ethical Ideal of Plutarch and the Greeks of the First Century A.D.* (Cincinnati, 1906), pp. 65–66.

22. *Plutarch's Moralia,* Vol. IX, trans. Edwin L. Minar, Jr., F. H. Sandbach, and W. C. Helmbold (1961).

Chapter Five

1. Representative critical opinion can be found in Richard C. Trench, *Plutarch* [:] *His Life, His Lives and His Morals* (London, 1873), p. 90; R. H. Barrow, *Plutarch and His Times* (London, 1967), p. 72; Ralph Waldo Emerson, "Introduction," *Plutarch's Miscellanies and Essays,* trans. William W. Goodwin (Boston, 1889), p. xi; and Edith Hamilton, *The Echo of Greece* (New York, 1957), p. 208.

2. In this connection, consult Barrow, p. 99; Robert Flacelière, *A Literary History of Greece* (Chicago, 1964), p. 357; J. P. Mahaffy, *The Greek World Under Roman Sway* (London and New York, 1890), p. 349; and Julian Hibbert, "A Life of Plutarchus" in *Plutarchus, and Theophrastus, On Superstition* (Kentish Town, England, 1828), pp. 14–16.

3. Barrow, p. 74.

4. *The Roman Questions of Plutarch,* trans. H. J. Rose (Oxford, 1924), p. 61.

5. Two books which amplify Plutarch's Platonism in detail are: Edmund G. Berry, *Emerson's Plutarch* (Cambridge, Mass., 1961) and R. M. Jones, *The Platonism of Plutarch* (Menasha, Wis., 1916). Very helpful, too, in the general area of Plutarch's religious convictions, is John Oakesmith's *The Religion of Plutarch* (London, 1902).

6. *A Short History of Greek Literature from Homer to Julian* (New York, Cincinnati, and Chicago, 1907), p. 483.

7. For a different viewpoint, see T. R. Glover, *The Conflict of Religions in the Early Roman Empire* (London, 1920), p. 110.

8. Glover, p. 93.

9. R. H. Barrow reinforces this point: "Plutarch could not have chosen a better word; for he means that Reason, working on the accumulated knowledge and experience of men will conduct a seeker up the steps towards an understanding of God and his Goodness; from that point Reason can take him no further; direct knowledge of God and communion with his spirit is for God and the soul" (p. 76).

10. Trench, p. 98. Mahaffy meanwhile misses the main point in asserting that Plutarch's ultimate goal was to make life more "agreeable" for men, since the balanced life Plutarch asks demands their involvement.

11. "Introduction" to *Plutarch's Lives,* trans. by Dryden, revised by A. H. Clough (New York, n.d.), pp. xxx–xxxi.

12. Mahaffy, p. 302.

13. "Demosthenes is right in declaring that the greatest safeguard States possess against tyrants is distrust . . ." (X. 28. 275, from *Precepts of Statecraft* in the *Moralia,* Vol. X).

14. *Paideia,* I, trans. Gilbert Highet, 2nd ed. (New York, 1960), 80.

15. Z. S. Fink, *The Classical Republicans,* 2nd ed. (Evanston, 1962), p .9.

16. T. A. Sinclair, *A History of Greek Political Thought* (London, 1959), p. 300.

17. See: Frederick M. Padelford, trans., *Essays on the Study and Use of Poetry by Plutarch and Basil the Great,* Yale Studies in English, XV (New York, 1902).

18. R. H. Barrow points out (on page 151), on the other hand, that Plutarch seemed singularly uninterested in Latin literature of any sort.

19. Phillip DeLacy, "Bibliography and Tragedy in Plutarch," *American Journal of Philology,* LXXIII, no. 2 (April, 1952), 161.

20. See: Roy C. Flickinger, *Plutarch as a Source of Information on the Greek Theater* (Chicago, 1904).

Chapter Six

1. J. A. K. Thomson, *The Classical Background of English Literature* (New York, 1962), p. 107.

2. Douglas Bush, *English Literature in the Earlier Seventeenth Century* [:] *1600–1660* (New York, 1952), p. 216. Hereafter cited as Bush.

3. This was true to an extraordinary degree in Elizabethan England. Consult, for instance: C. S. Lewis, *English Literature in the Sixteenth Century* (Oxford, 1954), p. 304. Hereafter noted as Lewis.

4. Bush, p. 182.

5. The seventeenth-century essay as a genre in England was particularly responsive to the shaping influences of Plutarch's commentaries. See: Elbert S. Thompson, *The Seventeenth-Century English Essay* (New York, 1967), p. 11.

6. Quoted by Ralph Waldo Emerson in his "Introduction" to *Plutarch's Miscellanies and Essays,* trans. revised by William W. Goodwin (Boston, 1889), p. x. Hereafter cited as Emerson, "Introduction."

7. Kingsley Martin, *French Liberal Thought in the Eighteenth Century,* ed. J. P. Mayer, 2nd ed., revised (London, 1954), pp. 147–48.

8. Oliver Goldsmith, "Preface" to *Plutarch's Lives,* found in *Collected Works of Oliver Goldsmith,* ed. Arthur Friedman, Vol. V (Oxford, 1966), footnote on p. 228.

9. *Holy Living and Dying* (London, 1897), pp. 142f.

10. Bush, pp. 314–15.

11. Kenneth B. Murdock, *Literature and Theology in Colonial New*

England (Cambridge, Mass., 1949), pp. 69–70. Hereafter cited as Murdock.

12. Murdock, p. 68, here is quoting from Mather's *Magnalia Christi Americana* of 1702.

13. *Ancilla to Classical Reading* (Morningside Heights, N. Y., 1961), p. 310.

14. *The Colloquies of Erasmus,* trans. Craig R. Thompson, Vol. I (Chicago and London, 1965), 76. Hereafter noted as *Colloquies.*

15. *Colloquies,* 454.

16. *Colloquies,* 267. For further exploration of Erasmus and Plutarch, see: Margaret M. Phillips, *The 'Adages' of Erasmus* (Cambridge, 1964).

17. Bush, pp. 210, 211.

18. *Essays,* Everyman's Library (London and New York, 1947), p. 52. Hereafter noted as Bacon, *Essays.*

19. Bacon, *Essays,* p. 122.

20. Lewis, p. 305.

21. J. H. Broome, *Rousseau* [:] *A Study of His Thought* (New York, 1963), p. 13.

22. Quoted in: Frances Winwar, *Jean-Jacques Rousseau* [:] *Conscience of An Era* (New York, 1961), p. 204. Also consult: Ronald Grimsley, *Jean-Jacques Rousseau* (Cardiff, 1961), pp. 36, 157, and 297.

23. Maturin Dréano, *La Pensée religieuse de Montaigne* (Paris, 1936), pp. 332–33. Hereafter cited as Dréano.

24. My own translation from: Pierre Villey, *Les Essais de Montaigne* (Paris, 1967), pp. 52, 53. For a thorough consideration of Montaigne and his reliance on Plutarch, see Villey's crucial study entitled *Les Sources et L'Evolution des Essais de Montaigne,* 2 vols. (Paris, 1908). Hereafter the former Villey book cited here will be noted as Villey, *Les Essais.*

25. My own translation from Villey, *Les Essais,* p. 55.

26. *Selected Essays of Montaigne in the Translation of John Florio,* ed. Walter Kaiser (Boston, 1964), p. 306.

27. My own translation from a quotation given in Villey, *Les Essais,* p. 60.

28. Dréano, p. 443.

29. A few helpful books regarding the inheritors of Plutarch's legacy are those of Bush and Thomson already cited in this chapter. In addition, see: Gilbert Highet, *The Classical Tradition* (London, Oxford, and New York, 1967).

30. Edmund G. Berry, *Emerson's Plutarch* (Cambridge, Mass., 1961), p. 24. Hereafter, this useful study will be noted as Berry.

31. R. C. Knight, *Racine et la Grèce* (Paris, 1950).

32. *A History of French Dramatic Literature in the Seventeenth Century. Part V. Recapitulation* [:] *1610–1700* (New York, 1966), 27.

33. Berry, p. 254. Also, consult: *The Early Lectures of Ralph Waldo Emerson,* Vol. I [1833–1836], eds. Stephen E. Whicher and Robert E. Spiller (Cambridge, Mass., 1959), 94–95. Hereafter this latter work will be cited as Whicher & Spiller.

34. Quoted in Berry, p. 285.

35. Emerson, "Introduction," p. xi.

36. Quoted in Berry, p. 270.

37. *The Complete Essays and Other Writings of Ralph Waldo Emerson,* ed. Brooks Atkinson (New York, 1950), pp. 228, 229. Also see: John S. Harrison, *The Teachers of Emerson* (New York, 1910), pp. 165–70.

38. Quoted in Berry, p. 256.

39. Quoted in Whicher & Spiller, II, 329. Also see Berry, p. 257.

40. Quoted in Berry, p. 278.

41. Whicher & Spiller, II, 175.

42. Emerson, "Introduction," p. xii.

43. More specifically, see: Skeat, "Introduction" to *Shakespeare's Plutarch, being a Selection from "The Lives" in North's Plutarch which Illustrate Shakespeare's Plays* (London and New York, 1892); Brooke, *Shakespeare's Plutarch,* 2 vols. (New York and London, 1909)—hereafter noted as Brooke; and Spencer, *Shakepeare's Plutarch* (Harmondsworth, England, 1964). Brooke, in addition, points out (II, xvi) that other Elizabethan drama aside from Shakespeare's similarly owed much to Plutarch.

44. *Life of Antony,* in *Plutarch's Lives,* Dryden translation (New York, n.d.), pp. 1118–19.

45. Brooke, II, xi.

46. *The Comparison of Demetrius and Antony,* in *Plutarch's Lives,* Dryden translation (New York, n.d.), pp. 1154, 1155.

47. As reproduced in the facsimile of the *Lives* printed by Shakespeare Head Press and published by Basil Blackwell (Oxford, 1928).

48. Albin Lesky, *A History of Greek Literature,* trans. James Willis & Cornelis de Heer (New York, 1966), p. 821.

49. The literary excitement generated by a single new find with respect to an author whose works have nearly become extinct is epitomized by Warren E. Blake's "Introduction" (p. i) to his edition of Menander's newly located play *Dyscolus* (Philological Monographs [Bronx, N. Y., 1966]) in which he writes of the manuscript that it "is probably the most important Greek literary discovery thus far in the century."

50. Berry, pp. 3f.

Selected Bibliography

PRIMARY SOURCES
(*modern translations in English*)

BABBITT, FRANK C. *et al.* (trans.). *Moralia.* 15 vols. Loeb Classical Library Series. London and Cambridge, Mass., 1927– . Once this Loeb version of the *Moralia* is completed—12 of the 15 volumes are published now—it will stand as the most authoritative translation in English. In the Loeb arrangement, the Greek text faces its corresponding English translation, page by page.

CLOUGH, A. H. (ed. and revis.). *Plutarch's Lives. The Translation called Dryden's.* "Introduction" by J. and W. Langhorne. New York, n.d. For many years, Dryden's translation of the *Lives* remained the most popular one in English. The "Introduction" in this volume written by the Langhorne brothers is of value for the interesting biographical remarks offered about Plutarch, as well as for the critical commentary concerning the *Lives.*

DRYDEN, JOHN (trans.); A. H. Clough (revis.). *Plutarch* [:] *The Lives of the Noble Grecians and Romans.* Modern Library Giant series. New York, n.d. All the *Lives* are incorporated into this single large volume which is one of the best-selling versions on the market today.

GOODWIN, WILLIAM W. (revis. trans.). *Plutarch's Miscellanies and Essays.* "Introduction" by Ralph Waldo Emerson. Boston, 1889. The most noteworthy feature of this edition is Emerson's illuminating "Introduction."

HADAS, MOSES. (trans.). *On Love, the Family, and the Good Life: Selected Essays of Plutarch.* New York, 1957. Professor Hadas brought together into this slim paperback edition several of Plutarch's most popular essays from the *Moralia.*

PERRIN, BERNADOTTE (trans.). *The Parallel Lives.* 11 vols. Loeb Classical Library Series. London and Cambridge, Mass., 1914–26. For the time-being this Loeb version remains the definitive one for the *Lives,* again with the English translation facing the original Greek text, page by page.

———. *Plutarch's Themistocles and Aristides.* New York and London,

1901. Miss Perrin here concentrates on two *Lives* only, giving a full introduction regarding the issues involved, as well as detailed notes.

PRICKARD, A. O. (trans.). *Selected Essays of Plutarch.* Vol. II. Oxford, 1918. The translator deals with only some of Plutarch's pieces here.

ROSE, H. J. (trans.), with Introductory Essays and a running commentary. *The Roman Questions of Plutarch.* Oxford, 1924. The renowned classicist Rose focuses on a small segment of the *Moralia* here, the *Roman Questions.* Nonetheless, this portion is of extreme interest to readers because of the fascinating view of mores from antiquity which it offers.

TURNER, PAUL (trans. and ed.). *Selected Lives from the Lives of the Noble Grecians and Romans.* Vol. I. Fontwell, England, 1963. This volume is composed of a selection of Plutarch's *Lives* in a very attractive format.

WYAT, THOMAS. (trans.). *Plutarch's Quyete of Mynde.* "Introduction" by Charles Read Baskervill. Reproduced in facsimile from a copy in the Henry E. Huntington Library (San Marino, Cal.). Baskervill's Introduction is particularly useful.

SECONDARY SOURCES

(Selected materials pertaining to Plutarch, his times, and viable evidence of his sustained influence in the world.)

ALTICK, RICHARD D. *Lives and Letters* [:] *A History of Literary Biography in England and America.* New York, 1965. A thoughtful survey of the status and shape of biography with some treatment of Plutarch's trail-blazing in the art of biography.

BACON, FRANCIS. *Essays.* Everyman's Library. London and New York, 1947. A perusal of Bacon's *Essays*—their topics and forms—reveals his debt to Plutarch.

BACON, HELEN H. *Barbarians in Greek Tragedy.* New Haven, 1961. A consideration of varying definitions of the "barbarian" in ancient Greece, as seen in drama.

BARKER, ERNEST. *From Alexander to Constantine.* Oxford, 1956. A broad survey of the most crucial centuries of classical Greece and Rome.

BARR, STRINGFELLOW. *The Mask of Jove* [:] *A History of Graeco-Roman Civilization from the Death of Alexander to the Death of Constantine.* Philadelphia and New York, 1966. A sensitive rendering of an epochal era that included Plutarch's lifetime.

BARROW, R. H. *Plutarch and His Times.* London, 1967. The best all-around treatment of Plutarch in English in almost one hundred years. By no means exhaustive in its coverage of the Greek's writings, Barrow nonetheless employs his fine sense of the Hellenistic and Roman eras to convey the ethos into which Plutarch was born and took part.

BERRY, EDMUND G. *Emerson's Plutarch.* Cambridge, Mass., 1961. Berry's work establishes a standard for anyone attempting to trace the influence of one writer upon another in a distant age; the book is all-encompassing in its scope and detailed to an extraordinary degree.

BOYD, C. E. *Public Libraries and Literary Culture in Ancient Rome.* Chicago, 1915. A useful examination of the intellectual climate in Rome, including the years when Plutarch visited and lectured there.

BROOKE, C. F. TUCKER (ed.). *Shakespeare's Plutarch.* 2 vols. New York and London, 1909. A long-time classic setting down Shakespeare's important borrowings from the Greek.

BROOME, J. H. *Rosseau* [:] *A Study of His Thought.* New York, 1963. Broome's scrutiny of Rousseau takes into account the Frenchman's close knowledge of and appreciation for Plutarch.

BUSH, DOUGLAS. *English Literature in the Earlier Seventeenth Century* [:] *1600–1660.* New York, 1952. Professor Bush's splendid survey displays, in passing, how many English writers of the time had read and digested Plutarch's works.

CURTIUS, ERNEST ROBERT. *European Literature and the Latin Middle Ages.* Trans. by Willard R. Trask. New York, 1963. Although not a prominently publicized author during the Middle Ages, Plutarch nevertheless did not drop from sight altogether, a fact shown in this book.

DELACY, PHILLIP. "Biography and Tragedy in Plutarch," *American Journal of Philology,* LXXIII (April, 1952), 159–71. A penetrating look at the esthetics involved in recounting the lives of great men, as explored by an outstanding classicist.

DELUNA, B. N. *Jonson's Romish Plot* [:] *A Study of "Catiline" and Its Historical Context.* Oxford, 1967. Here, Mrs. DeLuna seeks to reveal a lively religious controversy reflected in Ben Jonson tragegy. At the same time, readers are informed of Jonson's wholesale borrowings from Plutarch's accounts of Catiline as found in his *Life of Cicero.*

DRACHMANN, A. B. *Atheism in Pagan Antiquity.* London, 1922. Drachmann's work, although not recent, remains a very informative source for religious feelings in classical times.

DRÉANO, MATURIN. *La Pensée religieuse de Montaigne.* Paris, 1936. Montaigne's lifelong respect for Plutarch's writings surfaces clearly in this study.

EDEL, LEON. "A Proud Papa Speaks Up," *Book Week* (March 21,

1965), 2. The foremost biographer in America in our age defends here the very real contribution biography has to offer society; and much of what he says pertains to Plutarch's biographical pieces, as well.

EMERSON, RALPH WALDO. *The Complete Essays and Other Writings of Ralph Waldo Emerson*. Ed. Brooks Atkinson. New York, 1950. Emerson acknowledges his debts to Plutarch in his essays, frequently by name. The affinities are strong ones.

ERASMUS. *The Colloquies of Erasmus*. Trans. Craig R. Thompson. Vol. I. Chicago and London, 1965. Erasmus here refers to Plutarch as his mentor.

FERMOR, PATRICK LEIGH. *Roumeli* [:] *Travels in Northern Greece*. London, 1966. Fermor's travel account unearths specimens of the Romanizing of ancient Greece which can be found yet today.

FINK, Z. S. *The Classical Republicans* [:] *An Essay in the Recovery of a Pattern of Thought in Seventeenth-Century England*. Second ed. Evanston, Ill., 1962. A clear-cut example of how Plutarch's *Life of Lycurgus* eventually had an impact on political theorists centuries later.

FINLEY, M. I. Review of: R. H. Barrow, *Plutarch and His Times* (Indiana University Press, 1967), found in *The New York Review of Books*, IX (September 14, 1967), 29–31. The learned classicist Finley carefully sorts through Barrow's book on Plutarch here, making clear, all the while, that as an historian he holds little respect for Plutarch's accounts.

FLACELIÈRE, ROBERT. *Daily Life in Greece at the Time of Pericles*. Trans. by Peter Green. New York, 1965. An authoritative book by a French classicist which can make for an interesting comparison with Plutarch's picture of Greece's days of highest glory.

———. *A Literary History of Greece*. Trans. by Douglas Garman. Chicago, 1964. A sensitive survey of Greece's finest authors, including Plutarch.

FLICKINGER, ROY CASTON. *Plutarch as a Source of Information on the Greek Theater*. Doctoral Dissertation at the University of Chicago. Chicago, 1904. Flickinger, a world-renowned authority on ancient Greek theater, here reveals that Plutarch did not provide much help in that area.

GIANAKARIS, C. J. "The Legacy of Plutarch," *Western Humanities Review*, XXII (Summer, 1968), 207–13. A brief survey of Plutarch and his achievements.

GLOVER, T. R. *The Conflict of Religions in the Early Roman Empire*. 9th ed. London, 1920. An informative study of the varieties of religious beliefs in existence during Plutarch's general lifetime.

GOLDSMITH, OLIVER. Preface to *Plutarch's Lives, Abridged from the*

ORIGINAL GREEK, *Illustrated with* NOTES *and* REFLECTIONS, as found in *Collected Works of Oliver Goldsmith*, ed. Arthur Friedman, Vol. V. Oxford, 1966. Goldsmith's Preface is valuable in that it represents the orthodox view of the eighteenth-century English intellectual of Plutarch.

GRIMSLEY, RONALD. *Jean-Jacques Rousseau* [:] *A Study in Self-Awareness*. Cardiff, 1961. Another close scrutiny of Rousseau that reveals his agreement with Plutarch's general views on life.

HADAS, MOSES. "The Religion of Plutarch," *The South Atlantic Quarterly*, XLVI (1947), 84–92. The late Professor Hadas in this essay brilliantly sets forth the humanism that underlay Plutarch's alleged religious beliefs.

HADZSITS, GEORGE DEPUE. *Prolegomena to a Study of the Ethical Ideal of Plutarch and of the Greeks of the First Century A.D.* Doctoral Dissertation at the University of Michigan. Cincinnati, 1906. A splendid examination of the conventional moral attitudes of the Greeks of the time, including discussion of their view of God both as a singular and multiple entity.

HALEWOOD, WILLIAM H. "Plutarch in Houyhnhnmland: A Neglected Source for Gulliver's Fourth Voyage," *Philological Quarterly*, XLIV (April, 1965), 185–94. Halewood focuses on the travel traditions epitomized in several of Plutarch's essays in the *Moralia* and connects those traditions to Swift.

HAMILTON, EDITH. *The Echo of Greece*. New York, 1957. A standard book for capturing the sense of glory once enjoyed by Greece, as well as an exploration of that land after its decline.

HIBBERT, JULIAN. "A Life of Plutarchus," in *Plutarchus, and Theophrastus on Superstition*. Kentish Town, Great Britain, 1828. Though not at all authoritative, the life Hibbert furnishes is unique in many details, thus providing a provocative observation of Plutarch not found elsewhere.

HIGHET, GILBERT. *The Classical Tradition: Greek and Roman Influences in Western Literature*. New York, 1966. An essential book for anyone interested in classical letters; an impressive compendium of borrowings from antiquity as they are found in more recent literatures.

HUTTON, JAMES. *The Greek Anthology in Italy to the Year 1800*. Cornell Studies in English, XXIII. Ithaca, N. Y., 1935. An interesting work that suggests the great significance of Plutarch as a transmission agent throughout history for ancient knowledge and literature.

JACK, IAN. *English Literature 1815–1832*. Oxford, 1963. Professor Jack touches upon some English authors of the nineteenth century who borrowed from Plutarch in various ways.

JAEGER, WERNER. *Paideia: The Ideals of Greek Culture.* Trans. by Gilbert Highet. 3 vols. Second ed. New York, 1960. Indispensable volumes for anyone hoping to capture the essence of ancient Greek culture, especially where ethics are concerned.

JEBB, RICHARD C. "Literature" (Chapter III) in *A Companion to Greek Studies.* Ed. Leonard Whibley. Third ed. Cambridge, 1916. The celebrated classical scholar Jebb offers perceptive comments on Plutarch in this standard reference work.

JONES, A. H. M. *The Greek City from Alexander to Justinian.* Oxford, 1940. Mr. Jones's book affords the reader a better understanding of Plutarch's loyalty to his little home town by explaining the importance of the city unit in antiquity.

JONES, R. M. *The Platonism of Plutarch.* Doctoral Dissertation at the University of Chicago. Menasha, Wis., 1916. A very helpful study of Plutarch's own debt to Plato for many philosophical positions.

KENDALL, PAUL MURRAY. *The Art of Biography.* New York, 1965. Professor Kendall provides a fine history of the biographical form, while at the same time he delineates its unique attributes as a literary hybrid.

KNIGHT, ROY-C. *Racine et la Grèce.* Paris, 1950. Racine, Knight shows, knew Plutarch's writings well and drew from them frequently in his drama.

LANCASTER, HENRY CARRINGTON. *A History of French Dramatic Literature in the Seventeenth Century. Part V, Recapitulation 1610–1700.* New York, 1966. This authority of French letters documents here the innumerable borrowings from Plutarch by the French neo-classical playwrights.

LESKY, ALBIN. *A History of Greek Literature.* Trans. by James Willis and Cornelis de Heer. New York, 1966. Although the scope of this history is very broad, it also is very detailed, thanks to Lesky's painstaking treatment of all the important Greek authors.

LEVER, KATHERINE. *The Art of Greek Comedy.* London, 1956. Plutarch wrote prodigiously on many topics—but not much about the Greek theater. Miss Lever's book picks up the few references Plutarch does make about comedy.

LEWIS, C. S. *English Literature in the Sixteenth Century.* Oxford, 1954. Lewis' book, a standard study for students of Renaissance letters in England, documents in passing the enormous influence of Plutarch, both directly and indirectly, during that age.

MAHAFFY, J. P. *The Greek World Under Roman Sway: from Polybius to Plutarch.* London and New York, 1890. Mahaffy's penetrating look at Greece when Rome reigned supreme in the world suffers only from his strongly opinionated views of the leaders and authors of the time.

MALLINGER, JEAN. *Les Secrets Esotériques dans Plutarque*. Paris, 1946. The reader concerned with Plutarch who can handle French must turn to Mallinger's work to gain a perspective of the Greek's mind scarcely touched by scholars working in English.

MARTIN, KINGSLEY. *French Liberal Thought in the Eighteenth Century*. Ed. J. P. Mayer. Second ed., revis. London, 1954. Martin's book reflects the curious phenomenon of Plutarch, a Greek writing centuries earlier, influencing political thought in a modern, enlightened France.

MATHER, COTTON. *Bonifacius* [:] *An Essay Upon the Good*. Ed. David Levin. Cambridge, Mass., 1966. Mather's essay displays acknowledged debts to notions promulgated by Plutarch; at the same time, we thus are shown that Plutarch crossed the Atlantic early in America's history and became part of the moral fabric of the fledgling nation.

MONTAIGNE, M. *Selected Essays of Montaigne in the Translation of John Florio*. Ed. Walter Kaiser. Boston, 1964. The essays included here are enough to reveal Montaigne's admitted love of Plutarch's writings.

MURDOCK, KENNETH B. *Literature and Theology in Colonial New England*. Cambridge, Mass., 1949. Murdock's excellent survey pinpoints Plutarch's great attraction to the morally concerned preachers and authors in early America.

MURRAY, GILBERT. *A History of Ancient Greek Literature*. London, 1907. A foremost classicist of our era provides in this book his perceptive judgments about the finest Greek writings from antiquity; and Plutarch receives high praise from Murray as a master from the Greek past.

OAKESMITH, JOHN. *The Religion of Plutarch*. London, 1902. Using internal evidence from Plutarch's own works, principally the *Moralia*, Oakesmith documents the most probable position held by the Greek regarding religion.

PADELFORD, FREDERICK MORGAN (trans. and ed.). *Essays on the Study and Use of Poetry by Plutarch and Basil the Great*. Yale Studies in English, XV. New York, 1902. Padelford's commentaries on his topic are valuable, not only for the intelligent conclusions regarding Plutarch's attitudes toward poetry and the arts, but also for the general remarks Padelford offers concerning the customs and thought in Plutarch's age.

PARKE, H. W., and D. E. W. WORMELL. *The Delphic Oracle*. 2 vols. Oxford, 1956. Fascinating and essential volumes for an understanding of the Delphic oracles before Plutarch's time and also during his tenure as a temple priest.

PHILLIPS, MARGARET M. *The 'Adages' of Erasmus*. Cambridge, 1964. A scanning of Erasmus' *Adages* clearly reveals the author's affinities to Plutarch.

"Plutarch," in *Great Books of the Western World*, Vol. 14 (Encyclopaedia Britannica). Unadorned facts about Plutarch and his works.

"Plutarch," in *Oxford Classical Dictionary*, 1949 ed. A reasonable summary of Plutarch, his life, and the textual history of his writings.

RIST, MARTIN. *Two Isiac Mystics: Plutarch the Theologian and Apuleius the Priest*. Doctoral Dissertation at the University of Chicago. Chicago, 1936. By mining Plutarch's *Moralia*, particularly the *Isis and Osiris*, Rist establishes a convincing case for Plutarch's personal mysticism.

"Romios and Hellene," *Times Literary Supplement*, No. 3, 358 (July 7, 1966), 585–87. An informative account of Greece after centuries of Roman rule, reflecting the dissolution of Greece's once-proud spirit.

ROSTOVTZEFF, M. *The Social and Economic History of the Hellenistic World*. 3 vols. Oxford, 1941. No one hoping to comprehend the world in which Plutarch lived can avoid reading Rostovtzeff's masterful study. Though long, the work commands our interest, thanks to the intriguing material concerned and the splendid writing style.

SATIN, JOSEPH. *Shakespeare and His Sources*. Boston, 1966. Satin here, as other scholars of Shakespeare have done, documents closely what materials Shakespeare turned to when writing his plays; Plutarch is the seminal source for Shakespeare's Roman dramas, it is shown.

SHULMAN, ROBERT. "Melville's 'Timoleon': From Plutarch to the Early Stages of *Billy Budd*," *Comparative Literature*, XIX (Fall, 1967), 351–61. Plutarch's influence is shown to turn up in curious places. Here, Professor Shulman explores Melville's poem "Timoleon," showing that the author used Plutarch's *Lives* to aid him in clarifying his feelings about his own career, family, and beliefs.

SINCLAIR, T. A. *A History of Greek Political Thought*. London, 1959. Sinclair examines the connection between monotheism and monarchy in ancient Greece, a connection which Plutarch apparently believed in.

SKEAT, WALTER W. (ed.) *Shakespeare's Plutarch, being a Selection from The Lives in North's Plutarch which Illustrate Shakespeare's Plays*. London and New York, 1892. Skeat's early pace-setting work makes the comparison of Shakespeare's Roman dramas with their bases in Plutarch's accounts an easy task.

SPENCER, T. J. B. , ed. *Shakespeare's Plutarch.* Harmondsworth, England, 1964. Spencer in his book does what Tucker Brooke and Skeat had done before, that is to provide a text of the *Lives* by Plutarch which Shakespeare drew upon for several of his plays. Spencer's version, however, is wholly up to date and has the benefit of his firm grounding in Shakespeare which makes the comparisons he draws convincing and helpful.

STARR, CHESTER G. *Civilization and the Caesars.* Ithaca, New York, 1954. Professor Starr writes strictly as an historian; this volume as a result is most valuable for the excellent study of the ethos of the times when the Caesars ruled, thus furnishing another reference point for Plutarch's commentaries.

TARN, W. W. *Hellenistic Civilisation.* Third ed. London, 1951. An outstanding historian, Tarn offers here a close look at the Hellenistic milieu.

TAYLOR, HENRY OSBORN. *The Classical Heritage of the Middle Ages.* New York, 1963. Traces of Plutarch's writing and thought surface occasionally in medieval Europe, as Taylor reveals.

TENNEY, FRANK *et al. An Economic Survey of Ancient Rome.* 5 vols. and Index. Baltimore, 1933–40. For readers concerned strictly with Plutarch, Tenney's impressive work carries most value as establishing Plutarch's listeners as special aristocrats when he lectured in Rome on two separate occasions.

TETEL, MARCEL. *Rabelais.* Twayne World Authors Series. New York, 1967. An investigation into Rabelais' life reveals that he, too, read and concurred with many of Plutarch's concepts.

THOMPSON, ELBERT. *The Seventeenth-Century English Essays.* New York, 1967. Plutarch's influence as a writer of both casual and didactic essays has a significant effect on subsequent eras, as discussed in this book.

THOMSON, J. A. K. *The Classical Background of English Literature.* New York, 1962. As the title implies, Thomson, a very learned classicist, displays the continual and heavy borrowing from the classics to be found in all of English letters; and Plutarch was one of the most borrowed from of all.

———. *Classical Influences on English Prose.* New York, 1962. The author makes clear here that Plutarch remained for all later generations of writers an indispensable storehouse for anecdotes from antiquity. This is an extremely useful work.

TRACY, H. L. "Notes on Plutarch's Biographical Method," *The Classical Journal,* XXXVII (1941–42), 213–21. Tracy analyzes the artistic criterion Plutarch employed when gathering his materials to write down one of his lives.

TRENCH, RICHARD C. *Plutarch* [:] *His Life, His Lives and His Morals.*

London, 1873. Until Barrow's recent book, Trench's study of Plutarch had been the most exhaustive and understanding available in English for almost one hundred years. Clearly, Trench loved Plutarch; yet he brought to this study an honest appraisal of the man and his work. Still an outstanding book.

WHICHER, STEPHEN E., and ROBERT E. SPILLER (eds.). *The Early Lectures of Ralph Waldo Emerson. Vol. I, 1833–1836*. Cambridge, Mass., 1959. The Emersonian writings brought together reveal their author's indebtedness to Plutarch, especially in matters concerning deism.

WILLIAMSON, GEORGE. *The Senecan Amble*. Chicago, 1951. Although concentrating on Seneca's carryover into later writing mannerisms in the essay form, Williamson also touches upon Plutarch's effects as well on style.

WRIGHT, F. A. *A History of Later Greek Literature*. New York, 1932. A fair and straightforward rendering of literary history during part of Greece's history under the Romans.

WRIGHT, WILMER CAVE. *A Short History of Greek Literature from Homer to Julian*. New York, Cincinnati, and Chicago, 1907. A competent survey of the best Greek literature during its classical age.

Index